070.1

I BN

1 1 0492982 5

NEWSPAPERS

Ferguson
An imprint of Infobase Publishing

Careers in Focus: Newspapers

Ferguson
An imprint of Infobase Publishing
132 West 31st Street
New York NY 10001

Library of Congress Cataloging-in-Publication Data

Careers in focus. Newspapers.
    p.cm.
  Includes index.
  ISBN-13: 978-0-8160-6573-8
  ISBN-10: 0-8160-6573-X
  1. Journalism—Vocational guidance. I. J.G. Ferguson Publishing Company.
II. Title: Newspapers.
  PN4797.C37 2007
  070.4'023—dc22

Ferguson books are available at special discounts when purchased in bulk quantities for businesses, associations, institutions, or sales promotions. Please call our Special Sales Department in New York at (212) 967-8800 or (800) 322-8755.

You can find Ferguson on the World Wide Web at http://www.fergpubco.com

Text design by David Strelecky
Cover design by Salvatore Luongo

Printed in the United States of America

MP MSRF 10 9 8 7 6 5 4 3 2 1

This book is printed on acid-free paper.

Table of Contents

Introduction

Newspapers provide details, explanations, and interpretations of current events in all areas of society, such as politics, entertainment, and international affairs. For hundreds of years, they have provided timely, and sometimes urgent, information to the U.S. public. Despite the emergence of television and radio broadcasting and the Internet, newspapers still play an important role in American society. In fact, 85 percent of adults read a newspaper or visit a newspaper's Web site each week, according to *Time* magazine.

Circulation for newspapers ranges from a few thousand or less for a local community paper in rural Iowa, for example, to more than two million for national publications such as *USA Today*. Additionally, there are special interest newspapers for banking, business, fashion, law, labor, medicine, real estate, home furnishings, petroleum, and other industries. Ethnic newspapers (including African American, German, Greek, Japanese, Chinese, Polish, and Spanish) number in the hundreds.

Computer technology has had a dramatic impact on the newspaper industry. Many newspapers have Web sites that provide some or all of the information that appears simultaneously in print versions. These Web sites also allow newspapers to provide readers with the most current information in advance of the next printed edition. The Internet also allows reporters to research information, confirm stories, and communicate with relevant parties faster than they ever imagined. It also practically eliminates the lag time between the occurrence of a news event and the opportunity for the public to read about it. Reporters and editors now transmit stories by e-mail and the Internet. Computer-fed phototypesetters produce articles and headlines in "cold" (film) type at a rate of 2,000 lines a minute; whole pages are beamed by satellite in a matter of seconds to printing plants half a nation away.

Nearly 375,000 people are employed in the newspaper industry in occupations ranging from reporter, editor, and online producer; to advertising sales agent, media buyer, and marketing specialist; to office clerk, printing press operator, and delivery driver.

According to the *Career Guide to Industries* (published by the U.S. Department of Labor), employment in the publishing industry, including newspapers, is expected to grow more slowly than the average for all industries through 2014. This is mainly due to corporate mergers and increased efficiency of publishing operations, which results in a need for fewer employees.

The number of daily papers has gradually decreased over the past several years, and while most major cities could support two daily papers in the past, only about 40 cities today have competing papers. This decline is partly due to the growing competition from the Internet, television, and radio as up-to-the-minute news sources. There is also strong competition between papers for a limited number of local advertisers who may not have the funds or the desire to advertise in two publications. Despite these declines, newspaper advertising still generates more than $48 billion annually, according to *Time* magazine. To increase revenue and circulation, some newspapers are creating new design formats, launching Spanish-language editions and free digest spin-offs for commuters and special demographic groups (such as Generation Y), and interacting more with readers via blogs and other methods.

Due to industry consolidation, finding a reporting job on a daily newspaper has become tougher and tougher, as many dailies have folded. The best opportunities for reporters in the next decade will be found on newspapers in smaller towns and suburbs, both dailies and weeklies, where both populations and circulation are growing. Some major U.S. newspaper companies are expanding their operations overseas, particularly in Europe and Asia. More and more publications are producing online versions, which will require editors, writers, and salespeople, with skills specific to Web development.

Each article in *Careers in Focus: Newspapers* discusses a particular newspaper-related career in detail. The articles appear in Ferguson's *Encyclopedia of Careers and Vocational Guidance,* but have been updated and revised with the latest information from the U.S. Department of Labor, professional organizations, and other sources. The following paragraphs detail the sections and features that appear in the book.

The **Quick Facts** section provides a brief summary of the career including recommended school subjects, personal skills, work environment, minimum educational requirements, salary ranges, certification or licensing requirements, and employment outlook. This section also provides acronyms and identification numbers for the following government classification indexes: the Dictionary of Occupational Titles (DOT), the Guide to Occupational Exploration (GOE), the National Occupational Classification (NOC) Index, and the Occupational Information Network (O*NET)-Standard Occupational Classification System (SOC) index. The DOT, GOE, and O*NET-SOC indexes have been created by the U.S. government; the NOC index is Canada's career classification system. Readers can use the identification numbers listed in the Quick Facts section to access further information about a career. Print editions of the DOT

O*NET Dictionary of Occupational Titles. Indianapolis, Ind.: JIST Works, 2004) and GOE (The Complete Guide for Occupational Exploration. Indianapolis, Ind.: JIST Works, 1993) are available at libraries. Electronic versions of the NOC (http://www23.hrdc-drhc. gc.ca) and O*NET-SOC (http://online.onetcenter.org) are available on the Internet. When no DOT, GOE, NOC, or O*NET-SOC numbers are present, this means that the U.S. Department of Labor or Human Resources Development Canada have not created a numerical designation for this career. In this instance, you will see the acronym "N/A," or not available.

The **Overview** section is a brief introductory description of the duties and responsibilities involved in this career. Oftentimes, a career may have a variety of job titles. When this is the case, alternative career titles are presented.

The **History** section describes the history of the particular job as it relates to the overall development of its industry or field.

The **Job** describes the primary and secondary duties of the job.

Requirements discusses high school and postsecondary education and training requirements, any certification or licensing that is necessary, and other personal requirements for success in the job.

Exploring offers suggestions on how to gain experience in or knowledge of the particular job before making a firm educational and financial commitment. The focus is on what can be done while still in high school (or in the early years of college) to gain a better understanding of the job.

The **Employers** section gives an overview of typical places of employment for the job.

Starting Out discusses the best ways to land that first job, be it through the college placement office, newspaper ads, or personal contact.

The **Advancement** section describes what kind of career path to expect from the job and how to get there.

Earnings lists salary ranges and describes the typical fringe benefits.

The **Work Environment** section describes the typical surroundings and conditions of employment—whether indoors or outdoors, noisy or quiet, social or independent. Also discussed are typical hours worked, any seasonal fluctuations, and the stresses and strains of the job.

The **Outlook** section summarizes the job in terms of the general economy and industry projections. For the most part, Outlook information is obtained from the U.S. Bureau of Labor Statistics and is supplemented by information taken from professional associations. Job growth terms follow those used in the *Occupational*

Outlook Handbook. Growth described as "much faster than the average" means an increase of 27 percent or more. Growth described as "faster than the average" means an increase of 18 to 26 percent. Growth described as "about as fast as the average" means an increase of 9 to 17 percent. Growth described as "more slowly than the average" means an increase of 0 to 8 percent. "Decline" means a decrease by any amount.

Each article ends with **For More Information,** which lists organizations that provide information on training, education, internships, scholarships, and job placement.

Careers in Focus: Newspapers also includes photographs, informative sidebars, and interviews with professionals in the field.

Art Directors

OVERVIEW

In the newspaper industry, *art directors* work with artists, photographers, illustrators, desktop publishing specialists, and text and photo editors to develop visual images and generate copy. They are responsible for evaluating existing illustrations and photographs, choosing new illustrations and photographs, determining presentation styles and techniques, hiring both staff and freelance talent, working with layouts, and preparing budgets.

Art directors are also employed by advertising agencies to oversee the creation of an advertisement or ad campaign, television commercials, posters, and packaging, as well as in film and video and on the Internet.

In sum, art directors are charged with informing and educating consumers. They supervise both in-house and off-site staff, handle executive issues, and oversee the entire artistic production process. There are approximately 71,000 art directors working in the United States. About 5,000 of this total work in newspaper, book, and directory publishing.

QUICK FACTS

School Subjects
Art
Computer science

Personal Skills
Artistic
Communication/ideas

Work Environment
Primarily indoors
Primarily one location

Minimum Education Level
Bachelor's degree

Salary Range
$36,610 to $63,950 to
$125,890+

Certification or Licensing
None available

Outlook
About as fast as the average

DOT
164

GOE
01.02.03

NOC
5131

O*NET-SOC
27-1011.00

HISTORY

Artists have always been an important part of the creative process throughout history. Medieval monks illuminated their manuscripts, painting with egg-white tempera on vellum. Each copy of each book had to be printed and illustrated individually.

Printed illustrations first appeared in books in 1461. Through the years, prints were made through woodblock, copperplate, lithography, and other means of duplicating images. Although making many copies of the same illustration was now possible, publishers

5

still depended on individual artists to create the original works. Text editors usually decided what was to be illustrated and how, while artists commonly supervised the production of the artwork.

The first art directors were probably staff illustrators for book publishers. As the publishing industry grew more complex and incorporated new technologies such as photography and film, art direction evolved into a more supervisory position and became a full-time job. Publishers and advertisers began to need specialists who could acquire and use illustrations and photos. Women's magazines, such as *Vogue* and *Harper's Bazaar*, and photo magazines, such as *National Geographic*, relied so much on illustration and photography that the photo editor and art director began to carry as much power as the text editor. As newspapers added more sections and developed more creative designs, art directors also began to be in demand at newspapers.

Today's art directors supervise almost every type of visual project produced. Through a variety of methods and media, from newspapers and comic books to magazines and the Internet, art directors communicate ideas by selecting and supervising every element that goes into the finished product.

THE JOB

Art directors are responsible for all visual aspects of printed or on-screen projects. Art directors, even those with specialized backgrounds, must be skilled in and knowledgeable about design, illustration, photography, computers, research, and writing in order to supervise the work of graphic artists, photographers, illustrators, desktop publishing specialists, text and photo editors, and other employees.

In newspaper publishing, art directors may begin with the editorial department's concept or develop one in collaboration with these and other publishing professionals. Once the concept is established, art directors need to decide on the most effective way to communicate it by asking a variety of questions. What is the overall tone of the publication? (Serious? Thought-provoking? Comedic?) How will the illustrations complement the text? If only a small amount of text is being used, how will the illustrations be used to communicate information to the reader? What type of format (print or online or both) will be used? Additionally, if an article or feature is being revised, existing illustrations must be reevaluated.

After deciding what needs to be illustrated, art directors must find sources that can create or provide the art. Photo agencies, for example, have photographs and illustrations on thousands of different subjects. If, however, the desired illustration does not exist, it may have to be commissioned or designed by one of the staff designers or illustrators.

Commissioning artwork means that the art director contacts a photographer or illustrator and explains what is needed. A price is negotiated, and the artist creates the image specifically for the art director.

Once the illustrations and other art elements have been secured, they must be presented in an appealing manner. The art director supervises (and may help in the production of) the layout of the piece and presents the final version to the editorial director. Laying out is the process of figuring out where every image, headline, and block of text will be placed on the page. The size, style, and method of reproduction must all be specifically indicated so that the image is recreated as the director intended it.

Technology has been playing an increasingly important role in the art director's job. Most art directors, for example, use a variety of computer software programs, including Adobe InDesign, FrameMaker, Illustrator, and Photoshop; QuarkXPress; and CorelDRAW. Many others create and oversee Web sites for publishers and work with other interactive media and materials, including CD-ROM, touch screens, multidimensional visuals, and new animation programs.

Art directors usually work on more than one project at a time and must be able to keep numerous, unrelated details straight. They often work under pressure of a deadline and yet must remain calm and pleasant when dealing with staff and managers. Because they are supervisors, art directors are often called upon to resolve problems, not only with projects but with employees as well.

Art directors are not entry-level workers. They usually have years of experience working at lower-level jobs in the field before gaining the knowledge needed to supervise projects. Art directors in the newspaper industry have to know how printing presses operate and how content is created and layed out for online publications. They should also be familiar with a variety of production techniques in order to understand the wide range of ways that images can be manipulated to meet the needs of a project.

REQUIREMENTS

High School

A college degree is usually a requirement for art directors; however, in some instances, it is not absolutely necessary. A variety of high school courses will give you both a taste of college-level offerings and an idea of the skills necessary for art directors on the job. These courses include art, drawing, art history, graphic design, illustration, photography, advertising, and desktop publishing.

Math courses are also important. Most of the elements of sizing an image involve calculating percentage reduction or enlargement of the original picture. This must be done with a great degree of accuracy if the overall design is going to work.

Other useful courses that you should take in high school include business, computing, drama, English, technical drawing, cultural studies, psychology, and social science. Working on your school newspaper or yearbook will also give you a good introduction to this field.

Postsecondary Training

According to the American Institute of Graphic Arts, nine out of 10 artists have a college degree. Among them, six out of 10 have majored in graphic design, and two out of 10 have majored in fine arts. In addition, almost two out of 10 have a master's degree. Along with general two- and four-year colleges and universities, a number of professional art schools offer two-, three-, or four-year programs with such classes as figure drawing, painting, graphic design, and other art courses, as well as classes in art history, writing, business administration, communications, and foreign languages.

Courses in journalism, advertising, marketing, photography, layout, desktop publishing, and fashion are also important for those interested in becoming art directors. Specialized courses, sometimes offered only at professional art schools, may be particularly helpful for students who want to go into art direction. These include typography, animation, storyboard, Web site design, and portfolio development.

Because of the rapidly increasing use of computers in design work, it is essential to have a thorough understanding of how computer art and layout programs work. At smaller newspapers, the art director may be responsible for operating this equipment; at larger newspapers, a staff person, under the direction of the art director, may use these programs. In either case, the director must know what can be done with the available equipment.

In addition to coursework at the college level, many universities and professional art schools offer graduates or students in their final year a variety of workshop projects, desktop publishing training opportunities, and internships. These programs provide students with opportunities to develop their personal design styles as well as their portfolios.

Other Requirements

The work of an art director requires creativity, imagination, curiosity, and a sense of adventure. Art directors must be able to work with all sorts of specialized equipment and computer software, such as graphic design programs, as well as make presentations on the ideas behind their work.

The ability to work well with different people and organizations is a must for art directors. They must always be up-to-date on new techniques, trends, and attitudes. And because deadlines are a constant part of the work, an ability to handle stress and pressure well is key.

Other requirements for art directors include time management skills and an interest in media and people's motivations and lifestyles.

EXPLORING

High school students can get an idea of what an art director does by working on the staff of the school newspaper, magazine, or yearbook, and developing their own Web sites or zines. It may also be possible to secure a part-time job assisting the advertising director of your local newspaper or to work at an advertising agency. Developing your own artistic talent is important, and this can be accomplished through self-training (reading books and practicing); through courses in painting, drawing, or other creative arts; or by working with a group of friends to create a publication. At the very least, you should develop your "creative eye," that is, your ability to develop ideas visually. One way to do this is by familiarizing yourself with great works, such as paintings or highly creative magazines, books, motion pictures, videos, or commercials.

EMPLOYERS

Approximately 71,000 art directors are employed in the United States; about 5,000 of this total work in newspaper, book, and directory publishing. A variety of organizations in virtually all industries employ art directors. They might work at publishing houses, advertising agencies, museums, packaging firms, photography studios, marketing and public relations firms, desktop publishing outfits, digital prepress houses, or printing companies.

STARTING OUT

Since an art director's job requires a great deal of experience, it is usually not considered an entry-level position. Typically, a person on a career track toward art director is hired as an assistant to an established director. Recent graduates wishing to enter the field should have a portfolio containing samples of their work to demonstrate their understanding of both the business and the media in which they want to work.

Serving as an intern is a good way to get experience and develop skills. Graduates should also consider taking an entry-level job in a publisher's art department to gain initial experience. Either way, aspiring art directors must be willing to acquire their credentials by working on various projects. This may mean working in a variety of areas, such as advertising, marketing, editing, and design.

ADVANCEMENT

Many people who get to the position of art director do not advance beyond the title but move on to work at more prestigious newspapers and magazines. Competition for positions at well-known newspapers and magazines continues to be keen because of the sheer number of talented people interested. At smaller publications, the competition may be less intense, since candidates are competing primarily against others in the local market.

Other Opportunities in the Newspaper Industry

The newspaper industry offers a variety of career paths to people from all educational backgrounds. Here are just a few of the additional options not covered in this book:

- Accountants and auditors
- Intellectual property lawyers
- Computer software engineers
- Advertising and promotions managers
- Business managers
- Sales managers
- Computer programmers
- Computer and Internet security specialists
- Webmasters
- Desktop publishers
- Web developers
- Customer service representatives
- Circulation workers
- Promotions workers
- General maintenance mechanics
- Office clerks
- Bookkeeping, accounting, and auditing clerks
- Telemarketers
- Delivery drivers
- Security workers
- Sales representatives
- Data entry and information processing workers
- Mail clerks and mail machine operators
- Laborers

EARNINGS

According to the U.S. Department of Labor, beginning art directors or an art director who worked at a small firm earned $36,610 or less per year in 2005; experienced art directors working at larger companies earned more than $125,890. Mean annual earnings for art directors employed in newspaper, book, and directory publishing were $63,640 in 2005. Most companies employing art directors offer insurance benefits, a retirement plan, and other incentives and bonuses. Freelance art directors are usually responsible for providing their own health insurance and other benefits.

WORK ENVIRONMENT

Art directors usually work in studios or office buildings. While their work areas are ordinarily comfortable, well lit, and ventilated, they often handle glue, paint, ink, and other materials that pose safety hazards, and they should, therefore, exercise caution.

Art directors at art and design studios and publishing firms usually work a standard 40-hour week. Many, however, work overtime during busy periods in order to meet deadlines. While art directors work independently while reviewing artwork and reading copy, much of their time is spent collaborating with and supervising a team of employees, often consisting of copywriters, editors, photographers, graphic artists, and account executives.

OUTLOOK

The extent to which art director positions are in demand, like many other positions, depends on the economy in general; when times are tough, people and media companies spend less, and cutbacks are made. When the economy is healthy, employment prospects for art directors will be favorable. The U.S. Department of Labor predicts that employment for art directors will grow about as fast as the average for all other occupations through 2014. Publishers always want some type of illustration to enhance their newspapers, magazines, books, and Web sites. People who can quickly and creatively generate new concepts and ideas will be in high demand. However, it is important to note that the supply of aspiring artists is expected to exceed the number of job openings. As a result, those wishing to enter the field will encounter keen competition for salaried, staff positions as well as for freelance work. And although the Internet is expected to provide many opportunities for artists and art directors, some firms are hiring employees without formal art or design training to operate computer-aided design systems and oversee work.

FOR MORE INFORMATION

For more information on design professionals, contact
American Institute of Graphic Arts
164 Fifth Avenue
New York, NY 10010-5901
Tel: 212-807-1990
http://www.aiga.org

The Art Directors Club is an international, nonprofit organization of directors in advertising, graphic design, interactive media, broadcast design, typography, packaging, environmental design, photography, illustration, and related disciplines. For information, contact
The Art Directors Club
106 West 29th Street
New York, NY 10001-5301
Tel: 212-643-1440
Email: info@adcglobal.org
http://www.adcglobal.org

For information on the graphic arts, contact
Graphic Artists Guild
32 Broadway, Suite 1114
New York, NY 10004-1612
Tel: 212-791-3400
http://www.gag.org

For information on careers in newspapers and industry statistics, contact
Newspaper Association of America
4401 Wilson Boulevard, Suite 900
Arlington, VA 22203-1867
Tel: 571-366-1000
Email: IRC@naa.org
http://www.naa.org

For information on design issues in newspapers and other news publications, contact
Society for News Design
1130 Ten Rod Road, Suite D-202
North Kingstown, RI 02852-4180
Tel: 401-294-5233
http://www.snd.org

Cartoonists

OVERVIEW

Cartoonists are illustrators who draw pictures and cartoons to amuse, educate, and persuade people. They work for newspapers, magazines, cartoon syndicates, book publishers, and advertising agencies.

HISTORY

Broadly speaking, cartoons and other types of illustration have been used to educate and entertain people since the dawn of time. But it wasn't until the invention of movable metal type by Johannes Gutenberg in about 1450 that cartoons and other illustrations began to reach large audiences. The Protestant Reformer Martin Luther created illustrated pamphlets to convey his ideas about reforming the Roman Catholic Church, and distributed them to peasants, most of whom were illiterate. As people realized the power of images in educating the public and influencing their opinions, cartoons and other illustrations began to appear in printed publications throughout Europe.

In the United States, Benjamin Franklin's "Join, or Die" is considered the first political cartoon. Its depiction of a snake severed into eight segments was created to encourage the colonies to cooperate in dealing with the Iroquois Nation at the Albany Congress of 1754. By the Civil War, political cartoons had become increasingly important as a means of conveying opinions and information to the American public. Thomas Nast's pro-Union cartoons were so effective that President Abraham Lincoln called him the North's "best recruiting sergeant." Nast is best known, though, for his satirical cartoons in *Harper's Weekly* from 1869 to 1872 that spotlighted

Two cartoonists collaborate on a cartoon. *(Corbis)*

the abuses of power by William "Marcy" Tweed and his Tammany Hall political machine in New York City. When Tweed tried to elude justice by fleeing to Spain, it is said that authorities used Nast's cartoons to help identify Tweed.

In 1894, the continuity strip, which featured a comedic or dramatic story that continued from issue to issue, was invented as a means to boost newspaper circulation. By the late 1890s, newspaper magnates Joseph Pulitzer and William Randolph Hearst were using color comics as supplements in their Sunday papers to increase readership. In 1904, A. Piker Clerk, by Clare Briggs, became the first daily comic strip, and was soon followed by many other dailies. In 1912, William Randolph Hearst created the first syndication agency, which sold reprint rights for articles and comic strips to other newspapers in the United States and abroad. Today, this groundbreaking agency is known as the King Features Syndicate.

As cartoons grew in popularity, cartoonists realized that they needed organizations to represent their professional interests. In 1946, the National Cartoonists Society was founded. Today, it boasts a membership of 600 of the world's top cartoonists who specialize in creating editorial cartoons, humorous magazine and book illustrations, sports cartoons, comic strips, comic books, comic panels, animation, gag cartoons, greeting cards, and advertising. The Association of American Editorial Cartoonists (AAEC) was founded in 1957 to promote interest in editorial cartooning and represent the professional interests of editorial cartoonists. The AAEC has approximately 200 members.

THE JOB

Cartoonists draw illustrations for newspapers, magazines, books, greeting cards, and other publications. Cartoons most often are associated with newspaper comics or with editorial commentary, but they are also used to highlight and interpret information in publications as well as in advertising.

Whatever their individual specialty, cartoonists translate ideas onto paper in order to communicate these ideas to an audience. Sometimes the ideas are original; at other times they are directly related to the news of the day or to the content of a magazine article. After cartoonists come up with ideas, they discuss them with their employers, who include editors, art directors, or news directors. Next, cartoonists sketch drawings and submit these for approval. Employers may suggest changes, which the cartoonists then make. Cartoonists use a variety of art materials, including pens, pencils, markers, crayons, paints, transparent washes, and shading sheets. They may draw on paper, acetate, or bristol board.

Editorial cartoonists comment on society by drawing pictures with messages that are funny or thoughtful. They often use satire to illuminate the failings or foibles of public figures. Their drawings often depict political or social issues, as well as events in the worlds of sports and entertainment. *Portraitists* are cartoonists who specialize in drawing caricatures. Caricatures are pictures that exaggerate someone's prominent features, such as a large nose, to make them recognizable to the public. Most editorial cartoonists are also talented portraitists.

Comic strip artists tell jokes or short stories in newspapers and magazines with a series of pictures. Each picture is called a frame or a panel, and each frame usually includes words as well as drawings. *Comic book artists* also tell stories with their drawings, but their stories are longer, and they are not necessarily meant to be funny.

REQUIREMENTS

High School

If you are interested in becoming a cartoonist, you should, of course, study art in high school in addition to following a well-rounded course of study. To comment insightfully on contemporary life, it is useful to study political science, history, and social studies. English and communications classes will also help you to become a better communicator.

Postsecondary Training

Cartoonists need not have a college degree, but some art training is usually expected by employers. Typical college majors for those who attend college include art, communications, English, or liberal arts. Training in computers in addition to art can be especially valuable. If you are interested in becoming an editorial cartoonist, you should take courses in journalism, history, and political science.

Other Requirements

Cartoonists must be creative. In addition to having artistic talent, they must generate ideas, although it is not unusual for cartoonists to collaborate with writers for ideas. They must be able to come up with concepts and images to which the public will respond. They must have a good sense of humor and an observant eye to detect people's distinguishing characteristics and society's interesting attributes or incongruities.

EXPLORING

If you are interested in becoming a cartoonist, you should submit your drawings to your school paper. You also might want to draw posters to publicize activities, such as sporting events, dances, and meetings.

Student membership in professional associations is another good way to learn more about this career. The Association of American Editorial Cartoonists offers student membership to college students who create editorial cartoons on a regular basis for a college newspaper.

EMPLOYERS

Employers of cartoonists include newspapers, magazines, book publishers, cartoon syndicates, and advertising agencies. In addition, a number of these artists are self-employed, working on a freelance basis.

STARTING OUT

Formal entry-level positions for cartoonists are rare, but there are several ways for artists to enter the cartooning field. Most cartoonists begin by working piecemeal, selling cartoons to small publications, such as community newspapers, that buy freelance cartoons. Others assemble a portfolio of their best work and apply to publishers or the art departments of advertising agencies. In order to become established, cartoonists should be willing to work for what equals less than minimum wage.

ADVANCEMENT

Cartoonists' success, like that of other artists, depends on how much the public likes their work. Very successful cartoonists work for prestigious newspapers and magazines at the best wages; some become well-known to the public.

EARNINGS

Freelance cartoonists may earn anywhere from $100 to $1,200 or more per drawing, but top dollar generally goes only for big, full-color projects such as magazine cover illustrations. Most cartoonists average from $200 to $1,500 a week ($10,400 to $78,000 per year), although syndicated cartoonists on commission can earn much more. Salaries depend on the work performed. Although the U.S. Department of Labor does not give specific information regarding cartoonists' earnings, it does note that the mean earnings for salaried fine artists who worked for newspaper and book publishers were $46,280 in 2005. Salaried cartoonists, who are related workers, may have earnings similar to this figure.

Self-employed cartoonists do not receive fringe benefits such as paid vacations, sick leave, health insurance, or pension benefits. Those who are salaried employees of companies, agencies, newspapers, magazines, and the like do typically receive these fringe benefits.

WORK ENVIRONMENT

Most cartoonists work in big cities where employers such as magazine and newspaper publishers are located. They generally work in comfortable environments, at drafting tables or drawing boards with good light. Staff cartoonists work a regular 40-hour workweek but may occasionally be expected to work evenings and weekends to meet deadlines. Freelance cartoonists have erratic schedules, and the number of hours they work may depend on how much money they want to earn or how much work they can find. They often work evenings and weekends but are not required to be at work during regular office hours.

Cartoonists can be frustrated by employers who curtail their creativity, asking them to follow instructions that are contrary to what they would most like to do. Many freelance cartoonists spend a lot of time working alone at home, but cartoonists have more opportunities to interact with other people than do most working artists.

OUTLOOK

Employment for artists and related workers is expected to grow about as fast as the average for all occupations through 2014, according to the U.S. Department of Labor. Because so many creative and talented people are drawn to this field, however, competition for jobs will be strong.

More than 60 percent of all visual artists are self-employed, but freelance work can be hard to come by, and many freelancers earn little until they acquire experience and establish a good reputation. Competition for work will be keen; those with an undergraduate or advanced degree in art will be in demand. Experience in action drawing is a must. Additionally, cartoonists should have computer skills since their work is increasingly being featured on the Internet.

FOR MORE INFORMATION

For information on editorial cartooning, contact
Association of American Editorial Cartoonists
3899 North Front Street
Harrisburg, PA 17110-1583
Tel: 717-703-3069
http://editorialcartoonists.com

For education and career information, contact
National Cartoonists Society
1133 West Morse Boulevard, Suite 201
Winter Park, FL 32789-3727
Tel: 407-647-8839
Email: crowsegal@crowsegal.com
http://www.reuben.org

For career information, contact
Society of Illustrators
Museum of American Illustration
128 East 63rd Street
New York, NY 10021-7303

Tel: 212-838-2560
Email: info@societyillustrators.org
http://www.societyillustrators.org

To view a variety of editorial cartoons, visit
Daryl Cagle's Professional Cartoonists Index
http://www.cagle.com

Columnists

OVERVIEW

Columnists write opinion pieces for publication in newspapers or magazines. Some columnists work for syndicates, which are organizations that sell articles to many media at once.

Columnists can be generalists who write about whatever strikes them on any topic. Most columnists focus on a specialty, such as government, politics, local issues, health, humor, sports, gossip, or other themes.

Most newspapers employ local columnists or run columns from syndicates. Some syndicated columnists work out of their homes or private offices.

HISTORY

Because the earliest American newspapers were political vehicles, much of their news stories brimmed with commentary and opinion. This practice continued up until the Civil War. Horace Greeley, a popular editor who had regularly espoused partisanship in his *New York Tribune*, was the first to give editorial opinion its own page separate from the news.

As newspapers grew into instruments of mass communication, their editors sought balance and fairness on the editorial pages and began publishing a number of columns with varying viewpoints.

Famous Washington, D.C.-based columnist Jack Anderson was known for bringing an investigative slant to the editorial page. Art Buchwald and Molly Ivins became well known for their satirical look at government and politicians.

The growth of news and commentary on the Internet has only added to the power of columnists.

QUICK FACTS

School Subjects
Computer science
English
Journalism

Personal Skills
Communication/ideas
Helping/teaching

Work Environment
Indoors and outdoors
Primarily multiple locations

Minimum Education Level
Bachelor's degree

Salary Range
$18,300 to $32,270 to
$71,220+

Certification or Licensing
None available

Outlook
More slowly than the average

DOT
131

GOE
01.01.03

NOC
5123

O*NET-SOC
27-3022.00, 27-3043.00

THE JOB

Columnists often take news stories and enhance the facts with personal opinions and panache. Columnists may also write from their personal experiences. Either way, a column usually has a punchy start, a pithy middle, and a strong, sometimes poignant, ending.

Columnists are responsible for writing columns on a regular basis on accord with a schedule, depending on the frequency of publication. They may write a column daily, weekly, quarterly, or monthly. Like other journalists, they face pressure to meet a deadline.

Most columnists are free to select their own story ideas. The need to constantly come up with new and interesting ideas may be one of the hardest parts of the job, but also one of the most rewarding. Columnists search through newspapers, magazines, and the Internet, watch television, and listen to the radio. The various types of media suggest ideas and keep the writer aware of current events and social issues.

Next, they do research, delving into a topic much like an investigative reporter would, so that they can back up their arguments with facts.

Finally, they write, usually on a computer. After a column is written, at least one editor goes over it to check for clarity and correct mistakes. Then the cycle begins again. Often a columnist will write a few relatively timeless pieces to keep for use as backups in a pinch, in case a new idea can't be found or falls through.

Most columnists work in newsrooms or magazine offices, although some, especially those who are syndicated but not affiliated with a particular newspaper, work out of their homes or private offices. Many well-known syndicated columnists work out of Washington, D.C.

Newspapers often run small pictures of columnists, called head shots, next to their columns. This, and a consistent placement of a column in a particular spot in the paper, usually gives a columnist greater recognition than a reporter or editor.

REQUIREMENTS

High School

You'll need a broad-based education to do this job well, so take a college prep curriculum in high school. Concentrate on English and journalism classes that will help you develop research and writing skills. Keep your computer skills up to date with computer science courses. History, psychology, science, and math should round out your education. Are you interested in a particular topic, such as sports, politics, or developments in medicine? Then take classes that will help you develop your knowledge in that area. In the future, you'll be able to draw on this knowledge when you write your column.

Postsecondary Training

As is the case for other journalists, at least a bachelor's degree in journalism is usually required, although some journalists have earned degrees in political science or English. Experience may be gained by writing for the college or university newspaper and through a summer internship at a newspaper or other publication. It also may be helpful to submit freelance opinion columns to local or national publications. The more published articles, called "clips," you can show to prospective employers, the better.

Other Requirements

Being a columnist requires similar characteristics to those required for being a reporter: curiosity, a genuine interest in people, the ability to write clearly and succinctly, and the strength to thrive under deadline pressure. But as a columnist, you will also require a certain wit and wisdom, the compunction to express strong opinions, and the ability to take apart an issue and debate it.

EXPLORING

A good way to explore this career is to work for your school newspaper and perhaps write your own column. Participation in debate clubs will help you form opinions and express them clearly. Read your city's newspaper regularly, and take a look at national papers as well as magazines. Which columnists, on the local and national level, interest you? Why do you feel their columns are well done? Try to incorporate these good qualities into your own writing. Contact your local newspaper and ask for a tour of the facilities. This will give you a sense of what the office atmosphere is like and what technologies are used there. Ask to speak with one of the paper's regular columnists about his or her job. He or she may be able to provide you with valuable insights. Visit the Dow Jones Newspaper Fund Web site (http://djnewspaperfund.dow-jones.com/fund) for information on careers, summer programs, internships, and more. Try getting a part-time or summer job at the newspaper, even if it's just answering phones and doing data entry. In this way you'll be able to test out how well you like working in such an atmosphere.

EMPLOYERS

Newspapers of all kinds run columns, as do certain magazines and even public radio stations, where a tape is played over the airways of the author reading the column. Some columnists are self-employed, preferring to market their work to syndicates instead of working for a single newspaper or magazine.

STARTING OUT

Most columnists start out as reporters. Experienced reporters are the ones most likely to become columnists. Occasionally, however, a relatively new reporter may suggest a weekly column if the beat being covered warrants it, for example, politics.

Another route is to start out by freelancing, sending columns out to a multitude of newspapers and magazines in the hopes that someone will pick them up. Also, columns can be marketed to syndicates. A list of these, and magazines that may also be interested in columns, is provided in the *Writer's Market* (http://www.writersmarket.com).

A third possibility, one created by the emergence of the Internet, is simply beginning your own site or blog and using it to attract attention and thus jumpstart your career. Many who are well-known, such as Matt Drudge (http://www.drudgereport.com) and "Wonkette" (http://www.wonkette.com), started by beginning their own Web columns. If you get scoops, run interesting content, and people like what you have to say, you may find yourself with more readers than you can handle.

ADVANCEMENT

Newspaper columnists can advance in national exposure by having their work syndicated. They also may try to get a collection of their columns published in book form. Moving from a small newspaper or magazine to a large national publication is another way to advance.

Columnists also may choose to work in other editorial positions, such as editor, editorial writer or page editor, or foreign correspondent.

EARNINGS

Like reporters' salaries, the incomes of columnists vary greatly according to experience, newspaper size and location, and whether the columnist is under a union contract. But generally, columnists earn higher salaries than reporters.

The U.S. Department of Labor classifies columnists with news analysts, reporters, and correspondents, and reports that the median annual income for these professionals was $32,270 in 2005. Ten percent of those in this group earned less than $18,300, and 10 percent made more than $71,220 annually. According to the *Annual Survey of Journalism & Mass Communication Graduates,* directed by the University of Georgia, the median salary for those who graduated in 2005 with bachelor's degrees in journalism or mass communication was approximately $29,000. Those with master's degrees received average starting salaries of $37,000. Median earnings varied somewhat by employer; for example, those working for weekly papers earned somewhat less, while those working for consumer magazines earned somewhat more. Although these salary figures are for all journalists (not just columnists), they provide a general range for those working in this field. However, popular columnists at large papers earn considerably higher salaries.

Freelancers may get paid by the column. Syndicates pay columnists 40 percent to 60 percent of the sales income generated by their columns or a flat fee if only one column is being sold.

Freelancers must provide their own benefits. Columnists working on staff at newspapers and magazines receive typical benefits such as health insurance, paid vacation days, sick days, and retirement plans.

WORK ENVIRONMENT

Columnists work mostly indoors in newspaper or magazine offices, although they may occasionally conduct interviews or do research on location out of the office. Some columnists may work as much as 48 to 52 hours a week. Some columnists do the majority of their writing at home or in a private office, and come to the newsroom primarily for meetings and to have their work approved or changed by editors. The atmosphere in a newsroom is generally fast paced and loud, so columnists must be able to concentrate and meet deadlines in this type of environment.

OUTLOOK

The U.S. Department of Labor predicts that employment growth for news analysts, reporters, and correspondents (including columnists) will be slower than the average for all occupations through 2014. Growth will be hindered by such factors as mergers and closures of newspapers, decreasing circulation, and lower profits from advertising revenue. Online publications will be a source for new jobs. Competition for newspaper and magazine positions is very strong, and competition for the position of columnist is even stronger because these are prestigious jobs that are limited in number. Smaller daily and weekly newspapers may be easier places to find employment than major metropolitan newspapers, and movement up the ladder to columnist will also likely be quicker. Pay, however, is less than at bigger papers. Journalism and mass communication graduates will have the best opportunities, and writers will be needed to replace those who leave the field for other work or retire.

FOR MORE INFORMATION

For information on careers in newspaper reporting, education, and financial aid opportunities, contact
American Society of Journalists and Authors
1501 Broadway, Suite 302
New York, NY 10036-5505
Tel: 212-997-0947
http://www.asja.org

This association provides general educational information on all areas of journalism, including newspapers, magazines, television, and radio.
Association for Education in Journalism and Mass Communication
234 Outlet Pointe Boulevard
Columbia, SC 29210-5667
Tel: 803-798-0271
http://www.aejmc.org

For information on a career as a newspaper columnist, contact
National Society of Newspaper Columnists
PO Box 411532
San Francisco, CA 94141-1532
Tel: 866-440-6762
http://www.columnists.com

The SPJ has student chapters all over the United States and offers information on scholarships and internships.
Society of Professional Journalists (SPJ)
3909 North Meridian Street
Indianapolis, IN 46208-4011
Tel: 317-927-8000
http://www.spj.org

INTERVIEW

John von Rhein is a classical music critic for the Chicago Tribune. (To read his work, visit http://www.chicagotribune.com.) He discussed his work with the editors of Careers in Focus: Newspapers.

Q. Tell us about yourself.

A. I have been a full-time classical music critic since 1971, when I was hired by the *Akron Beacon Journal* as its music and dance critic. I have held the title of music critic at the *Chicago Tribune* since 1977. I also contribute articles to various national and international publications on a freelance basis.

Q. Why did you decide to enter this career?

A. In many ways the job chose me, rather than the other way around. I had originally wanted to become a professional violinist, playing in a symphony orchestra. Later I had hopes of becoming a music history teacher at the college level. But my lifelong interest in reading music reviews, plus encouragement from several newspaper critics of my acquaintance, convinced me I should pursue writing criticism for a profession.

Q. How did you train for this career? What was your educational path?

A. I never attended journalism school. All the training I received came on the job. I came to that job armed with what I learned from my undergraduate and graduate work as a dual major in music history and English (B.A. degrees in both subjects, University of California at Los Angeles and California State University at Los Angeles, with graduate studies in music at the latter university). I came armed with a solid working knowledge of the classical repertory by virtue of having been an avid record collector since my teens. My years of violin study paid off enormously as well, giving me a greater empathy for performers and insights into the psychology of musical performance than I would have had otherwise.

Q. How/where did you get your first job as a music critic?

A. I had had four or so years experience as an assistant (or "stringer") music critic for a newspaper in Southern California while taking classes at California State University-Los Angeles. I was weighing various career options after graduation when a critic-colleague told me of a job opening at the *Beacon Journal* in Ohio. Armed with my modest portfolio of clippings, I flew to

Akron, was interviewed, and hired. It was the proverbial "right place, right time" situation. But I also had the writing experience and qualifications the editors were looking for. Much the same could be said of my being hired by the *Chicago Tribune*.

Q. What is the most important piece of advice that you have to offer students as they graduate and look for jobs in this field?

A. Classical music criticism is an increasingly endangered species in today's shrinking newspaper market where good jobs are few in all areas of arts criticism, and where the validity of reviews (as opposed to feature stories, news stories, and personality pieces) is being questioned by editors desperately seeking ways to reverse declining readership. Classical music critics thus find themselves having to prove their "relevance" to a younger demographic that isn't interested in classical music and generally finds newspapers (print as well as online versions) irrelevant to their daily lives. It's not a healthy situation, and I'm not sanguine about the future of classical criticism in the daily press.

Q. What are the pros and cons of work as a music critic?

A. On the positive side, it's being paid to work in an art form that is self-renewing and endlessly rewarding. Writing about the artists who create, re-create, administer, and fund classical music enables you to influence public opinion, uphold performance standards in your community, and maintain classical music as a living art form. On the negative side, it's the issues I raised above. There's a lot more micromanaging by editors than when I began my career in newspapers—the "autonomy" of critics is today regarded as so Old Media. Sometime it's a real fight to get even basic coverage of the classical "beat" in the paper. There's never enough space, and one is constantly competing with pop culture writers for that finite space. Many editors (few of whom ever attend concerts) wonder why they should be giving so much attention to something relatively few readers care about.

necessary to provide clearly written, accurate reading material. Both positions tend to be entry-level jobs that may provide the opportunity for advancement. Editorial and research assistants may be assigned to support one editor or writer, an editorial team, or an entire department. They may work on one project at a time or several projects simultaneously.

Editorial assistants perform many different tasks. They may handle the clerical aspects of an editorial project, such as going through the editorial department mail, filing documents, making photocopies, corresponding with authors, and submitting expense reports and invoices to accounting for payment. They may be responsible for obtaining permission to reuse previously published materials such as artwork, maps, tables, or writing from another person, or verifying that the author has already obtained permission. They may also perform other tasks more directly involved with editing, such as reviewing text for style and format issues, correcting any spelling or grammar errors, and adding or deleting content to make the text more readable or to adhere to space specifications. They may be responsible for using desktop publishing software to take editorial elements such as text, photos, or art and create page layouts.

In addition to the tasks mentioned above, some editorial assistants who work with artists and photographers are responsible for writing captions for photographs or labels for artwork. Editorial assistants who work for newspapers may perform basic and formulaic tasks such as updating the winning lottery numbers, sports scores, or calendar events listed in the newspaper, or they may undertake simple writing assignments such as creating birth, engagement, wedding, or anniversary announcements, or obituaries. Editorial assistants who work for book publishers may be responsible for reading through unsolicited manuscripts from writers and determining which editor, if any, it should be forwarded to for further consideration.

Research assistants generally perform research tasks such as verifying the dates, facts, names of persons and places, and statistics used by a writer. They may review a writer's sources and then verify that the information provided by these sources is correct. They may contact any persons interviewed by the writer to ensure that any quotes used by the writer are truthful and correct. Research assistants also contact experts in subject areas pertaining to the topic of the article, often to obtain additional information for the writer, or verify information already used in the article. If a research assistant finds any errors or discrepancies with the writer's text, they are expected to flag and correct them. A research assistant may meet with the writer and/or editor to discuss any discrepancies that are not easily resolved.

Research assistants use a variety of tools to do their jobs. They rely on telephones, fax machines, and computers to obtain the information they need. Researchers may utilize libraries, the Internet, and in-house collections of information as sources of facts, figures, and statistics. Although they may work in a variety of settings, many research assistants work in the magazine/periodical publishing industry.

REQUIREMENTS

High School

Editorial and research assistants must be expert communicators, so you should excel in English. You must learn to write extremely well, since you will be correcting and even rewriting the work of others. If elective classes in writing are available in your school, take them. Take journalism and communications courses. Work as a writer or editor for the school paper. Since virtually all editorial and research assistants use computers, take computer courses and learn how to type quickly and accurately.

Postsecondary Training

Most employers require an editorial assistant to have at least two years of college, and a bachelor's degree is preferred, especially if you wish to advance to a higher position. Research assistants should also have a bachelor's degree. Most editorial workers have degrees in English or journalism, but it is not unheard of to major in one of the other liberal arts. If you know that you want to specialize in a specific field—for example, scientific editing—you may wish to major in an area of science while minoring in English, writing, or journalism. Many colleges offer courses in book editing, magazine design, general editing, and writing. Some colleges, such as the University of Chicago, University of Denver, and Stanford University, offer programs in publishing.

While in college, work on the school paper, literary magazine, or yearbook staff. Many magazines and newspapers offer internships to students interested in editorial work. Find a part-time job with a newspaper or magazine, even if it is a noneditorial position. Take advantage of these opportunities. Everything you can learn about the publishing business will help you find a job later.

Other Requirements

Good editorial and research assistants are fanatics for the written word. They read a lot, across many topics, and know how to think clearly and communicate what they are thinking. When they are

Summer Journalism Programs

If you are interested in a career in journalism, participating in a summer program offered by a college or university is a great way to learn more about the field. In these programs, you will get the chance to be taught by top journalism professors; learn to research and write stories, take photographs, lay out a newspaper, create a Web page, and countless other skills; tour newspaper newsrooms; listen to lectures from industry experts; and interact with students just like you who are interested in journalism. Most importantly, you will get a chance to try out a career in journalism before college. The following is a short list of summer journalism programs for high school students:

University of Alabama
Multicultural Journalism Workshop
205-348-8607
http://www.ccom.ua.edu/mjw/index.html

Arizona State University
Cronkite Summer Journalism Institute
480-965-5011
http://cronkite.asu.edu/beyond/hs.html

Colorado High School Press Association
Student Newspaper Camp
970-491-3757
http://chspa.colostate.edu/sumshops.cfm

University of Florida
Summer Journalism Institute

EARNINGS

Competition for editorial jobs is fierce, and there is no shortage of people who wish to enter the field. For that reason, companies that employ editorial and research assistants generally pay relatively low wages.

A *Publishers Weekly* salary survey reported that editorial assistant salaries in 2003 ranged from $28,378 at smaller companies to $30,400 at large publishing houses. However, beginning salaries of $20,000 or less are still common in many places.

Earnings of research assistants vary widely, depending on the level of education and the experience of the research assistant and employer. Generally, large companies pay research assistants more than smaller companies and nonprofit organizations do. Self-employed research

352-392-4186
http://www.jou.ufl.edu/sji

University of Iowa
Summer Journalism Workshops
319-335-3455
http://www.uiowa.edu/%7Ejournshp/ourworkshops/index.htm

Northwestern University
National High School Institute
800-662-6474
http://www.northwestern.edu/nhsi

Ohio University
High School Journalism Workshop
803-776-5354
http://www.scripps.ohiou.edu/workshop/hsjw.htm

Princeton University
Summer Journalism Program
http://www.princeton.edu/~sjp

Washington and Lee University
Summer Scholars
540-458-8727
http://summerscholars.wlu.edu

For a complete list of summer journalism programs, visit http://www.highschooljournalism.org.

assistants get paid by the hour or by assignment. Depending on the experience of the research assistant, the complexity of the assignment, and the location of the job, pay rates may be anywhere from $7 to $25 per hour, although $10 to $12 is the norm.

WORK ENVIRONMENT

The environments in which editorial and research assistants work can vary widely. For the most part, publishers of all kinds realize that a quiet atmosphere is conducive to work that requires tremendous concentration. Most editorial and research assistants work in cubicles. Editorial and research assistants in publishing often work in quieter surroundings than do assistants working for a newspaper

Fashion Illustrators and Photographers

OVERVIEW

Fashion illustrators and *photographers* work in the exciting world of fashion. Their artistic focus is specifically on styles of clothing and personal image. Illustrators use a variety of media (for example, pencil, pen and ink, or computer technology) to create illustrations that appear in print and electronic formats. Photographers take and develop pictures of people, places, and objects while using a variety of cameras and photographic equipment. Both the illustrations and the photographs are used to advertise new fashions, promote models, and popularize designers.

HISTORY

Illustration featured prominently in the ancient civilizations of Mesopotamia, Egypt, and later Greek and Roman civilizations. Drawings depicting knowledge and conveying ideas have also been found among ancient Assyrian, Babylonian, Egyptian, and Chinese societies. Modern illustration began during the Renaissance of the 15th and 16th centuries, with the work of Leonardo da Vinci, Andreas Vesalius, and Michelangelo Buonarotti.

Over time, tools have been developed to aid illustrators in their work. Illustrators have made use of parallel bars, compasses, French curves, and Tsquares, but the development of computer technology has largely replaced these mechanical tools with software

Postsecondary Training

Although this is a career in which you don't need to take a specific postsecondary educational route, there are a number of options available to you. There are, for example, academic programs in fashion illustration and photography at many colleges, universities, and adult education centers. Some community and junior colleges offer associate's degrees in photography or commercial art. An advantage to pursuing education beyond high school is that it gives you an opportunity to build a portfolio, which is a collection of an artist's best sketches or photos that shows prospective clients a variety of skills. In addition to studying art and photography, it is advantageous to study clothing construction, fabrics, fashion design, or cosmetology.

Photography studies will include shooting and processing techniques using both black-and-white and color film, digital technology, lighting, and composition. Illustration studies will include drawing, painting, layout, color, and design.

Other Requirements

Both illustrators and photographers need excellent manual dexterity, good eyesight and color vision, and artistic ability. They need an eye for composition as well as the ability to work creatively with their chosen medium. Because both of these jobs involve working with groups of people, illustrators and photographers need to be patient, accommodating, and professional. An eye for detail is essential. And, naturally, they should be interested in fashion and expressing style through images.

EXPLORING

You can explore this field by taking drawing and photography classes both at school and through local organizations such as community centers. Also, consider joining a school photography or art club. These clubs will give you the opportunity to meet with others who share your interests, and they sometimes sponsor talks or meetings with professionals. Join the staff of the school yearbook, newspaper, or literary magazine. These publications often make use of visual art to accompany their text. Look for part-time or summer work at a camera store or art supply store, or assisting a professional artist or photographer. This work experience will give you the opportunity to become familiar with many "tools of the trade." Explore your interest in the fashion field by reading fashion magazines that will keep you up to date on fashion trends, models, and photographers' and illustrators' work. Try drawing or sewing your own fashion creations. If you can't find work at a camera or art store, try getting a job at a clothing store. This will give you experience working with people and clothes, and you might even be able to suggest fashion advice to customers.

EMPLOYERS

More than half of all professional photographers and visual artists (which includes illustrators) are self-employed. Others work for large retailers, magazines, newspapers, design or advertising firms, and fashion firms (called *houses*).

STARTING OUT

If you have received a degree, one of the best ways to start out in this business is to find a job through your school's career services office or by networking with alumni. Those who are interested in photography sometimes gain entry by working as assistants or trainees to established photographers. You may be asked to do such things as move lights, work in the darkroom, and schedule appointments, but you will also gain experience and make contacts in the field. Those who are financially able may go into business for themselves right away. However, it may take considerable time to establish yourself in the field and have a business that is profitable. Illustrators sometimes start out receiving no pay for their work, just a byline (a credit giving the person's name). However, having your name published with your work will give you exposure on a professional level. As you take on more work, you may be able to begin charging more. Again, it may take some time to become established in the field.

ADVANCEMENT

Advancement for both fashion illustrators and photographers generally comes as they gain professional recognition. The freelance illustrator or photographer who becomes known for the creativity and high quality of his or her work will find that he or she has a growing clientele. More clients translate into more jobs; more jobs translate into higher earnings. In addition, as illustrators or photographers become better known, they can charge more for their services and be more selective about what jobs they take. Illustrators and photographers who are salaried employees of organizations may either move up within the organization, taking on supervisory roles or working with specific accounts for example, or they may have starting their own photography or illustration business as their ultimate goal.

newspapers, advertising firms, and fashion houses. The outlook for these agencies currently looks strong. The popularity of American fashions around the world should create a demand for illustrators and photographers. In addition, numerous outlets for fashion, such as e-zines and retail Web sites, will create a need for illustrators and photographers.

Competition for jobs, however, will be keen since these positions are highly attractive to people with artistic ability. In addition, the *Occupational Outlook Handbook* notes that the growing popularity of digital cameras and computer art programs can allow consumers and businesses to produce and access illustrations and photographic images on their own. Despite this improved technology, the specialized skills of the trained illustrator and photographer should still find demand in the fashion world. Individuals who are creative and persistent in finding job leads and who are able to adapt to rapidly changing technologies will be the most successful.

FOR MORE INFORMATION

The ASMP promotes the rights of photographers and photojournalists, educates its members in business practices, and promotes high standards of ethics.
American Society of Media Photographers (ASMP)
150 North Second Street
Philadelphia, PA 19106-1912
Tel: 215-451-2767
http://www.asmp.org

This organization is committed to improving conditions for all creators of graphic art and to raising standards for the entire industry.
Graphic Artists Guild
32 Broadway, Suite 1114
New York, NY 10004-1612
Tel: 212-791-3400
http://www.gag.org

The NPPA maintains a job bank, provides educational information, and makes insurance available to its members. It also publishes News Photographer *magazine.*
National Press Photographers Association (NPPA)
3200 Croasdaile Drive, Suite 306
Durham, NC 27705-2588
Tel: 919-383-7246

Email: info@nppa.org
http://www.nppa.org

This organization provides training, publishes its own magazine, and offers various services for its members.
Professional Photographers of America
229 Peachtree Street, NE, Suite 2200
Atlanta, GA 30303-1608
Tel: 800-786-6277
Email: csc@ppa.com
http://www.ppa.com

This national institution promotes and stimulates interest in the art of illustration by offering exhibits, lectures, educational programs, and social interchange.
Society of Illustrators
128 East 63rd Street
New York, NY 10021-7303
Tel: 212-838-2560
Email: info@societyillustrators.org
http://www.societyillustrators.org

This Web site allows you to browse through galleries of hundreds of established fashion photographers, as well as several illustrators.
FashionBook.com
http://fashionbook.com/home.html

Visit this site for more career advice
Fashion Net: How to Become a Fashion Photographer
http://www.fashion.net/howto/photography

The inventions of the telegraph, telephone, typewriter, portable typewriter, the portable laptop computer, and the Internet all have contributed to the field of foreign correspondence.

THE JOB

The foreign correspondent is stationed in a foreign country where his or her job is to report on the news there. Foreign news can range from the violent (wars, coups, and refugee situations) to the calm (cultural events and financial issues). Although a domestic correspondent is responsible for covering specific areas of the news, like politics, health, sports, consumer affairs, business, or religion, foreign correspondents are responsible for all of these areas in the country where they are stationed. A China-based correspondent, for example, could spend a day covering the new trade policy between the United States and China, and the next day report on the religious persecution of Christians by the Chinese government.

A foreign correspondent often is responsible for more than one country. Depending on where he or she is stationed, the foreign correspondent might have to act as a one-person band in gathering and preparing stories.

"There are times when the phone rings at five in the morning and you're told to go to Pakistan," said Michael Lev, a foreign correspondent reporting on the Far East for the *Chicago Tribune* and other newspapers. "You must keep your wits about you and figure out what to do next."

For the most part, Lev decides on his own story ideas, choosing which ones interest him the most out of a myriad of possibilities. But foreign correspondents alone are responsible for getting the story done, and unlike reporters back home, they have little or no support staff to help them. And just like other news reporters, foreign correspondents work under the pressure of deadlines. In addition, they often are thrown into unfamiliar situations in strange places.

Part of the importance of a foreign correspondent's job is keeping readers or viewers aware of the various cultures and practices held by the rest of the world. Lev says he tries to focus on similarities and differences between the Asian countries he covers and the United States. "If you don't understand another culture, you are more likely to come into conflict with it," he says.

Foreign correspondents are drawn to conflicts of all kinds, especially war. They may choose to go to the front of a battle to get an accurate picture of what's happening. Or they may be able to get the story from a safer position. Sometimes they even face weapons trained directly on them.

Much of a foreign correspondent's time is spent doing research, investigating leads, setting up appointments, making travel arrangements, making on-site observations, and interviewing local people or those involved in the situation. The foreign correspondent often must be experienced in taking photographs or shooting video.

Living conditions can be rough or primitive, sometimes without running water. The job can sometimes be isolating.

After correspondents have interviewed sources and noted observations about an event or filmed it, they put their stories together, writing on computers and using modern technology like the Internet, e-mail, satellite telephones, and fax machines to finish the job and transmit the story to their newspaper, broadcast station, or wire service. Many times, correspondents work out of hotel rooms.

REQUIREMENTS

High School

In addition to English and creative writing needed for a career in journalism, you should study languages, social studies, political science, history, and geography. Initial experience may be gained by working on your school newspaper or yearbook, or taking advantage of study-abroad programs.

Postsecondary Training

In college, pursuing a journalism major is helpful but may not be crucial to obtaining a job as a foreign correspondent. Classes, or even a major, in history, political science, or literature could be beneficial. Economics and foreign languages also help.

Other Requirements

To be a foreign correspondent, in addition to a definite love of adventure, you need curiosity about how other people live, diplomacy when interviewing people, courage to sometimes confront people on uncomfortable topics, the ability to communicate well, and the discipline to sometimes act as your own boss. You also need to be strong enough to hold up under pressure yet flexible enough to adapt to other cultures.

EXPLORING

Does this type of work interest you? To explore this field, you can begin by honing your skills in different journalism media. Join your high school newspaper staff to become a regular columnist or write special feature articles. Check out your high school's TV station and audition to be an anchor. Is there a radio station at your school? If so,

employment outlook is expected to remain relatively stable, or even increase should a major conflict or war occur.

Factors that keep the number of foreign correspondents low are the high cost of maintaining a foreign news bureau and the relative lack of interest Americans show in world news. Despite these factors, the number of correspondents is not expected to decrease. There are simply too few as it is; decreasing the number could put the job in danger of disappearing, which most journalists believe is not an option. For now and the near future, most job openings will arise from the need to replace those correspondents who leave the job.

FOR MORE INFORMATION

The ASJA promotes the interests of freelance writers. It provides information on court rulings dealing with writing issues, has a writers' referral service, and offers a newsletter.

American Society of Journalists and Authors (ASJA)
1501 Broadway, Suite 302
New York, NY 10036-5505
Tel: 212-997-0947
http://www.asja.org

This association provides the annual publication Journalism and Mass Communication Directory *with information on educational programs in all areas of journalism (newspapers, magazines, television, and radio).*

Association for Education in Journalism and Mass
   Communication
234 Outlet Pointe Boulevard
Columbia, SC 29210-5667
Tel: 803-798-0271
http://www.aejmc.org

The SPJ has chapters all over the United States. The SPJ's Web site offers career information and information on internships and fellowships.

Society of Professional Journalists (SPJ)
Eugene S. Pulliam National Journalism Center
3909 North Meridian Street
Indianapolis, IN 46208-4011
Tel: 317-927-8000
http://www.spj.org

Visit the following Web site for comprehensive information on journalism careers, summer programs, and college journalism programs.

High School Journalism
http://www.highschooljournalism.org

—————————— INTERVIEW ——————————

Laurie Goering is the Chicago Tribune's *Africa correspondent. (To read her work, visit http://www.chicagotribune.com/news/nation-world/chi-lauriegoering,0,5802085.storygallery.) Before working in Africa, she reported from a variety of countries throughout the world, including Cuba, Brazil, Mexico, Afghanistan, and Iraq. Laurie discussed her career with the editors of* Careers in Focus: Newspapers.

Q. Why did you decide to become a foreign correspondent?

A. I decided to become a journalist because I loved writing and thought it would be a way to make a career out of that love. In my 20s I had the opportunity to travel to Africa with my family and fell in love with the bigger world beyond the U.S. borders I'd known. That directed my general interest in writing and journalism toward being a foreign correspondent, as I couldn't wait to get back out to see more of the world.

Q. What is the most memorable story that you have covered as a foreign correspondent and why?

A. After more than a dozen years working as a foreign correspondent I've covered thousands of stories, many of them memorable. But covering the Second Gulf War in Iraq was unlike anything I'd done before in terms of danger and, in many ways, the importance of the story. Another story I particularly remember was about Suriname, a small South American country, preparing to grant huge logging concessions in its tropical rainforest, a huge threat to biodiversity in the country. After a Malaysian logging representative made clear his racism against the Surinamese people in an interview with me, the Surinamese government cancelled the logging concession and today that area is protected as national forest.

Q. What advice would you offer high school students who are interested in this career?

A. I think anyone who really wants to be any kind of journalist, not just a foreign correspondent, needs to get writing early, on a high

Computer technology has revolutionized the way many graphic designers do their work. Today it is possible to be a successful graphic designer even if you can't draw more than simple stick figures. Graphic designers are now able to draw, color, and revise the many different images they work with using computers. They can choose typefaces, size type, and place images without having to manually align them on the page using a T square and triangle. Computer graphics enable graphic designers to work more quickly, since details like size, shape, and color are easy to change.

Graphics design programs are continually revised and improved, moving more and more design work from the artist's table to the computer mousepad and graphics tablet. As computer technology continues to advance in the areas of graphics and multimedia, more designers will have to know how to work with virtual reality applications.

THE JOB

Graphic designers are not primarily fine artists, although they may be highly skilled at drawing or painting. Most designs commissioned to graphic designers involve both artwork and copy (words). Thus, the designer must not only be familiar with the wide range of art media (photography, drawing, painting, collage, etc.) and styles, but he or she must also be familiar with a wide range of typefaces and know how to manipulate them for the right effect. Because design tends to change in a similar way to fashion, designers must keep up to date with the latest trends. At the same time, they must be well grounded in more traditional, classic designs.

Graphic designers can work as *in-house designers* for a particular company, as *staff designers* for a graphic design firm, or as *freelance designers* working for themselves. Some designers specialize in designing advertising materials or packaging. Others focus on corporate identity materials such as company stationery and logos. Some work mainly for publishers, designing newspaper, book, and magazine covers and page layouts. Some work in the area of computer graphics, creating still or animated graphics for computer software, videos, or motion pictures. Depending on the project's requirements, some graphic designers work exclusively on the computer, while others may use both the computer and drawings or paintings created by hand.

Whatever the specialty and whatever their medium, all graphic designers take a similar approach to a project, whether it is for an entirely new design or for a variation on an existing one. Graphic designers begin by determining the needs and preferences of clients and potential users, buyers, or viewers.

For example, a graphic designer working on the redesign of the arts section of a newspaper will likely meet with editors of that section to discuss such points as the intended audience for the section; the combination of text, color, and graphics that will be used; new features that will be added to the section; and other topics. Project budgets must be respected: A design that may be perfect in every way but that is too costly to reproduce is basically useless. Graphic designers may need to compare their ideas with similar ones from other companies and analyze the image they project. They must have a good knowledge of how various colors, shapes, and layouts affect the viewer psychologically.

After a plan has been conceived and the details worked out, the graphic designer does some preliminary designs (generally two or three) to present to the client for approval. The client may reject the preliminary designs entirely and request a new one, or he or she may ask the designer to make alterations. The designer then goes back to the drawing board to attempt a new design or make the requested changes. This process continues until the client approves the design.

Once a design has been approved, the graphic designer prepares the piece for professional reproduction, or printing. The printer may require what is called a mechanical, in which the artwork and copy are arranged on a white board just as it is to be photographed, or the designer may be asked to submit an electronic copy of the design. Either way, designers must have a good understanding of the printing process, including color separation, paper properties, and halftone (photograph) reproduction.

REQUIREMENTS

High School
While in high school, take any art and design courses that are available. Computer classes are also helpful, particularly those that teach page layout programs or art and photography manipulation programs. Working on the school newspaper or yearbook can provide valuable design experience. You could also volunteer to design flyers or posters for school events.

Postsecondary Training
More graphic designers are recognizing the value of formal training; at least two out of three people entering the field today have a

EXPLORING

If you are interested in a career in graphic design, there are a number of ways to find out whether you have the talent, ambition, and perseverance to succeed in the field. Take as many art and design courses as possible while still in high school and become proficient at working on computers. To get an insider's view of various design occupations, you could enlist the help of art teachers or school guidance counselors to make arrangements to tour design firms and interview designers.

While in school, seek out practical experience by participating in school and community projects that call for design talents. These might include such activities as building sets for plays, setting up exhibits, planning seasonal and holiday displays, and preparing programs and other printed materials. If you are interested in publication design, work on the school newspaper or yearbook is invaluable.

Part-time and summer jobs are excellent ways to become familiar with the day-to-day requirements of a design job and gain some basic related experience. Possible places of employment include design studios, design departments in advertising agencies and manufacturing companies, department and furniture stores, flower shops, workshops that produce ornamental items, and museums. Museums also use a number of volunteer workers. Inexperienced people are often employed as sales, clerical, or general assistants; those with a little more education and experience may qualify for jobs in which they have a chance to develop actual design skills and build portfolios of completed design projects.

EMPLOYERS

Graphic designers hold approximately 228,000 jobs. The publishing industry—including book, magazine, newspaper, and newsletter publishers—is a primary employer of graphic designers. Additionally, designers work in many different industries, including the wholesale and retail trade (such as department stores, furniture and home furnishings stores, apparel stores, and florist shops); manufacturing industries (such as machinery, motor vehicles, aircraft, metal products, instruments, apparel, textiles, printing, and publishing); service industries (such as business services, engineering, and architecture); construction firms; and government agencies. Public relations and publicity firms, advertising agencies, and mail-order houses all have graphic design departments.

About 30 percent of all graphic designers are self-employed, a higher proportion than is found in most other occupations. These freelance designers sell their services to multiple clients.

STARTING OUT

The best way to enter the field of graphic design is to have a strong portfolio. Potential employers rely on portfolios to evaluate talent and how that talent might be used to fit the company's needs. Beginning graphic designers can assemble a portfolio from work completed at school, in art classes, and in part-time or freelance jobs. The portfolio should continually be updated to reflect the designer's growing skills so it will always be ready for possible job changes.

Those just starting out can apply directly to companies that employ designers. Many colleges and professional schools have placement services to help graduates find positions, and sometimes it is possible to get a referral from a previous part-time employer or volunteer coordinator.

ADVANCEMENT

As part of their on-the-job training, beginning graphic designers generally are given simpler tasks and work under direct supervision. As they gain experience, they move up to more complex work with increasingly less supervision. Experienced graphic designers, especially those with leadership capabilities, may be promoted to chief designer, design department head, or other supervisory positions.

Graphic designers with strong computer skills can move into other computer-related positions with additional education. Some may become interested in graphics programming in order to further improve their computer design capabilities. Others may want to become involved with multimedia and interactive graphics. Video games, touch screen displays in stores, and even laser light shows are all products of multimedia graphic designers.

When designers develop personal styles that are in high demand in the marketplace, they sometimes go into business for themselves. Freelance design work can be erratic, however, so usually only the most experienced designers with an established client base can count on consistent full-time work.

EARNINGS

The range of salaries for graphic designers is quite broad. Many earn as little as $20,000, while others make more than $110,000. Salaries depend primarily on the nature and scope of the employer. The U.S. Department of Labor reports that in 2005, graphic designers employed in newspaper, book, and directory publishing earned mean annual salaries of $36,850; the highest paid 10 percent of all

Learn More About It

Berry, John D. (ed.) *Contemporary Newspaper Design: Shaping the News in the Digital Age: Typography & Image on Modern Newsprint.* New York: Mark Batty Publisher, 2004.

Cox, Mary, and Michael Schweer. (eds.) *Artist's & Graphic Designer's Market 2007.* Cincinnati, Ohio: Writers Digest Books, 2006.

Fleishman, Michael. *Starting Your Career as a Freelance Illustrator or Graphic Designer.* New York: Watson-Guptill Publications, 2001.

Myers, Debbie Rose. *The Graphic Designer's Guide to Portfolio Design.* Hoboken, N.J.: Wiley, 2005.

Society for News Design. *The Best of Newspaper Design.* 27th ed. Gloucester, Mass.: Rockport Publishers, 2006.

graphic designers earned $67,660 or more, while the lowest paid 10 percent earned $23,160 or less.

The American Institute of Graphic Arts/Aquent Salary Survey 2006 reports that designers earned a median salary of $39,000 in 2006, while senior designers earned a median of $52,000 annually. Creative/design directors earned a median of $76,000 a year. The owner of a consulting firm can make $130,000 or more.

Self-employed designers can earn a lot one year and substantially more or less the next. Their earnings depend on individual talent and business ability, but, in general, are higher than those of salaried designers. Although like any self-employed individual, freelance designers must pay their own insurance costs and taxes and are not compensated for vacation or sick days.

Graphic designers who work for large corporations receive full benefits, including health insurance, paid vacation, and sick leave.

WORK ENVIRONMENT

Most graphic designers work regular hours in clean, comfortable, pleasant offices or studios. Conditions vary depending on the design specialty. Some graphic designers work in small establishments with few employees; others work in large organizations with large design departments. Some deal mostly with their coworkers; others may have a lot of public contact. Freelance designers are paid by the assignment. To maintain a steady income, they must constantly strive to please their clients and to find new ones. At times, graphic designers may have to work long, irregular hours in order to complete an especially ambitious project.

OUTLOOK

Employment for qualified graphic designers is expected to grow about as fast as the average for all occupations through 2014; employment should be especially strong for those involved with computer graphics and animation. As computer graphic and Web-based technology continues to advance, there will be a need for well-trained computer graphic designers. Companies that have always used graphic designers will expect their designers to perform work on computers. Companies for which graphic design was once too time consuming or costly are now sprucing up company newsletters and magazines, among other things, requiring the skills of design professionals.

Because the design field appeals to many talented individuals, competition is expected to be strong in all areas. Beginners and designers with only average talent or without formal education and technical skills may encounter some difficulty in finding a job.

FOR MORE INFORMATION

For more information about careers in graphic design, contact
American Institute of Graphic Arts
164 Fifth Avenue
New York, NY 10010-5901
Tel: 212-807-1990
http://www.aiga.org

Visit the NASAD's Web site for information on schools.
National Association of Schools of Art and Design (NASAD)
11250 Roger Bacon Drive, Suite 21
Reston, VA 20190-5248
Tel: 703-437-0700
Email: info@arts-accredit.org
http://nasad.arts-accredit.org

For information on design issues in newspapers and other news publications, contact
Society for News Design
1130 Ten Rod Road, Suite D-202
North Kingstown, RI 02852-4180
Tel: 401-294-5233
http://www.snd.org

To read an online newsletter featuring competitions, examples of top designers' work, and industry news, visit the SPD's Web site.

Society of Publication Designers (SPD)
17 East 47th Street, 6th Floor
New York, NY 10017-1920
Tel: 212-223-3332
Email: mail@spd.org
http://www.spd.org

Marketing Research Analysts

OVERVIEW

Marketing research analysts collect, analyze, and interpret data in order to determine potential demand for a product or service. By examining the buying habits, wants, needs, and preferences of consumers, research analysts are able to recommend ways to improve products, increase sales, and expand customer bases. There are approximately 190,000 marketing research analysts employed in the United States.

HISTORY

Knowing what customers want and what prices they are willing to pay have always been concerns of manufacturers and producers of goods and services. As industries have grown and competition for consumers of manufactured goods has increased, businesses have turned to marketing research as a way to measure public opinion and assess customer preferences.

Marketing research formally emerged in Germany in the 1920s and in Sweden and France in the 1930s. In the United States, emphasis on marketing research began after World War II. With a desire to study potential markets and gain new customers, U.S. firms hired marketing research specialists, professionals who were able to use statistics and refine research techniques to help companies reach their marketing goals. By the 1980s, research analysts could be found even in a variety of Communist countries, where the quantity of consumer goods being produced was rapidly increasing.

Today, the marketing research analyst is a vital part of the marketing team. By conducting studies and analyzing data, research professionals help companies address specific marketing issues and concerns.

THE JOB

Marketing researchers collect and analyze all kinds of information in order to help companies improve their products, establish or modify sales and distribution policies, and make decisions regarding future plans and directions. In addition, research analysts are responsible for monitoring both in-house studies and off-site research, interpreting results, providing explanations of compiled data, and developing research tools.

One area of marketing research focuses on company products and services. In order to determine consumer likes and dislikes, research analysts collect data on brand names, trademarks, product design, and packaging for existing products, items being test-marketed (such as a new daily newspaper for twenty somethings or a new Web site design for a media company), and those in experimental stages. Analysts also study competing products and services that are already on the market to help managers and strategic planners develop new products and create appropriate advertising campaigns.

In the sales methods and policy area of marketing research, analysts examine firms' sales records and conduct a variety of sales-related studies. For example, information on sales in various geographical areas is analyzed and compared to previous sales figures, changes in population, and total and seasonal sales volume. By analyzing this data, marketing researchers can identify peak sales periods and recommend ways to target new customers. Such information helps marketers plan future sales campaigns and establish sales quotas and commissions.

Advertising research is closely related to sales research. Studies on the effectiveness of advertising in different parts of the country are conducted and compared to sales records. This research is helpful in planning future advertising campaigns and in selecting the appropriate media to use.

Marketing research that focuses on consumer demand and preferences solicits opinions of the people who use the products or services being considered. For example, a marketing research analyst might survey readers of a daily newspaper to gauge their likes and dislikes regarding the design of the newspaper, favorite and least favorite sections, and the frequency of their visits to the newspaper's new Web site. In addition to actually conducting opinion studies, marketing researchers often design the ways to obtain the information. They write scripts for telephone interviews, develop direct-mail questionnaires and field surveys, and design focus group programs.

Through one or a combination of these studies, market researchers are able to gather information on consumer reaction to the need for and style, design, price, and use of a product. The studies attempt to reveal who uses various products or services, identify potential customers, or get suggestions for product or service improvement. This information is helpful for forecasting sales, planning design modifications, and determining changes in features.

Once information has been gathered, marketing researchers analyze the findings. They then detail their findings and recommendations in a written report and often orally present them to management as well.

A number of professionals compose the marketing research team. The *project supervisor* is responsible for overseeing a study from beginning to end. The *statistician* determines the sample size—or the number of people to be surveyed—and compares the number of responses. The project supervisor or statistician, in conjunction with other specialists (such as *demographers* and *psychologists*), often determines the number of interviews to be conducted as well as their locations. *Field interviewers* survey people in various public places, such as shopping malls, office complexes, and popular attractions. *Telemarketers* gather information by placing calls to current or potential customers, to people listed in telephone books, or to those who appear on specialized lists obtained from list houses. Once questionnaires come in from the field, *tabulators* and *coders* examine the data, count the answers, code noncategorical answers, and tally the primary counts. The marketing research analyst then analyzes the returns, writes up the final report, and makes recommendations to the client or to management.

Marketing research analysts must be thoroughly familiar with research techniques and procedures. Sometimes the research problem is clearly defined, and information can be gathered readily. Other times, company executives may know only that a problem exists as evidenced by a decline in sales. In these cases, the market research analyst is expected to collect the facts that will aid in revealing and resolving the problem.

REQUIREMENTS

High School

Most employers require their marketing research analysts to hold at least a bachelor's degree, so a college preparatory program is advised. Classes in English, marketing, economics, mathematics, psychology, and sociology are particularly important. Courses in computer science are especially useful, since a great deal of tabulation and statistical analysis is required in the marketing research field.

Postsecondary Training

A bachelor's degree is essential for careers in marketing research. Majors in marketing, business administration, statistics, computer science, history, or economics provide a good background for most types of research positions. In addition, course work in sociology and psychology is helpful for those who are leaning toward consumer demand and opinion research. Since quantitative skills are important in various types of industrial or analytic research, students interested in these areas should take statistics, econometrics, survey design, sampling theory, and other mathematics courses.

Many employers prefer that a marketing research analyst hold a master's degree as well as a bachelor's degree. A master's of business administration, for example, is frequently required on projects calling for complex statistical and business analysis. Graduate work at the doctorate level is not necessary for most positions, but it is highly desirable for those who plan to become involved in advanced research studies.

Other Requirements

To work in this career, you should be intelligent, detail oriented, and accurate; have the ability to work easily with words and numbers; and be particularly interested in solving problems through data collection and analysis. In addition, you must be patient and persistent, since long hours are often required when working on complex studies.

As part of the market research team, you must be able to work well with others and have an interest in people. The ability to communicate, both orally and in writing, is also important, since you will be responsible for writing up detailed reports on the findings in various studies and presenting recommendations to management.

EXPLORING

You can find many opportunities in high school to learn more about the necessary skills for the field of marketing research. For example, experiments in science, problems in student government, committee work, starting a literary journal or newsletter, and other school activities provide exposure to situations similar to those encountered by marketing research analysts.

You can also seek part-time employment as a survey interviewer at local marketing research firms. Gathering field data for consumer surveys offers valuable experience through actual contact with both the public and marketing research supervisors. In addition, many companies seek a variety of other employees to code, tabulate, and edit surveys; monitor telephone interviews; and validate the information entered on written questionnaires. You can search for job listings in local newspapers and on the Web or apply directly to research organizations.

EMPLOYERS

Approximately 190,000 marketing research analysts are employed in the United States. Marketing research analysts are employed by large corporations (including media companies), industrial firms, advertising agencies, data collection businesses, and private research organizations that handle local surveys for companies on a contract basis. While many marketing research organizations offer a broad range of services, some firms subcontract parts of an overall project out to specialized companies. For example, one research firm may concentrate on product interviews, while another might focus on measuring the effectiveness of product advertising. Similarly, some marketing analysts specialize in one industry or area. For example, print media marketing specialists prepare sales forecasts for newspaper and magazine publishers, which use the information in their advertising and sales programs.

Did You Know?

- Nearly 375,000 people were employed in the newspaper industry in 2004.
- The average nonsupervisory worker in the industry worked an average of 34.1 hours per week in 2004—slightly higher than the average (33.7) for workers in all industries.
- The average reader of a daily newspaper is male, white, college-educated, married, and a homeowner.
- 52 percent of Americans consider newspapers the most important tool for planning shopping excursions.
- Nearly 54 million people in the United States read an online newspaper in 2006.

Source: Newspaper Association of America

Although many smaller firms located all across the country out-source studies to marketing research firms, these research firms, along with most large corporations that employ marketing research analysts, are located in such big cities as New York or Chicago. Approximately 90 percent of salaried marketing research analysts are employed in private industry, but opportunities also exist in government and academia, as well as at hospitals, public libraries, and a variety of other types of organizations.

STARTING OUT

Students with a graduate degree in marketing research and experience in quantitative techniques have the best chances of landing jobs as marketing research analysts. Since a bachelor's degree in marketing or business is usually not sufficient to obtain such a position, many employees without postgraduate degrees start out as research assistants, trainees, interviewers, or questionnaire editors. In such positions, those aspiring to the job of research analyst can gain valuable experience conducting interviews, analyzing data, and writing reports.

Use your college career services office, the Web, and help wanted sections of local newspapers to look for job leads. Another way to get into the marketing research field is through personal and professional contacts. Names and telephone numbers of potential employers may come from professors, friends, or relatives. Finally, students who have participated in internships or have held marketing research-related jobs on a part-time basis while in school or during the summer may be able to obtain employment at these firms or at similar organizations.

ADVANCEMENT

Most marketing research professionals begin as *junior analysts* or *research assistants*. In these positions, they help in preparing questionnaires and related materials, training survey interviewers, and tabulating and coding survey results. After gaining sufficient experience in these and other aspects of research project development, employees are often assigned their own research projects, which usually involve supervisory and planning responsibilities. A typical promotion path for those climbing the company ladder might be from assistant researcher to marketing research analyst to assistant manager and then to manager of a branch office for a large private research firm. From there, some professionals become market research executives or research directors for industrial or business firms.

Since marketing research analysts learn about all aspects of marketing on the job, some advance by moving to positions in other departments, such as advertising or sales. Depending on the interests and experience of marketing professionals, other areas of employment to which they can advance include data processing, teaching at the university level, statistics, economics, and industrial research and development.

In general, few employees go from starting positions to executive jobs at one company. Advancement often requires changing employers. Therefore, marketing research analysts who want to move up the ranks frequently go from one company to another, sometimes many times during their careers.

EARNINGS

Beginning salaries in marketing research depend on the qualifications of the employee, the nature of the position, and the size of the firm. Interviewers, coders, tabulators, editors, and a variety of other employees usually get paid by the hour and may start at $6 or more per hour. The U.S. Department of Labor reported that in 2005, median annual earnings of market research analysts were $57,300. The middle 50 percent earned salaries that ranged from $41,370 to $81,970. Salaries ranged from less than $31,530 to more than $108,990. Experienced analysts working in supervisory positions at large firms can earn even higher earnings. Market research directors earn up to $200,000.

Because most marketing research workers are employed by business or industrial firms, they receive typical fringe benefit packages, including health and life insurance, pension plans, and paid vacation and sick leave.

WORK ENVIRONMENT

Marketing research analysts usually work a 40-hour week. Occasionally, overtime is necessary in order to meet project deadlines. Although they frequently interact with a variety of marketing research team members, analysts also do a lot of independent work, analyzing data, writing reports, and preparing statistical charts.

While most marketing research analysts work in offices located at the firm's main headquarters, those who supervise interviewers may go into the field to oversee work. In order to attend conferences, meet with clients, or check on the progress of various research studies, many market research analysts find that regular travel is required.

OUTLOOK

The U.S. Department of Labor predicts that employment for marketing research analysts will grow faster than the average for all occupations through 2014. Increasing competition among producers of consumer goods and services and industrial products, combined with a growing awareness of the value of marketing research data, will contribute to opportunities in the field. Opportunities will be best for those with graduate degrees who seek employment in marketing research firms, companies that design computer systems and software, financial services organizations, health care institutions, advertising firms, manufacturing firms that produce consumer goods, and insurance companies.

While many new graduates are attracted to the field, creating a competitive situation, the best jobs and the highest pay will go to those individuals who hold a master's degree or doctorate in marketing research, statistics, economics, or computer science.

FOR MORE INFORMATION

For information on college chapters, internship opportunities, and financial aid opportunities, contact
American Advertising Federation
1101 Vermont Avenue, NW, Suite 500
Washington, DC 20005-6306
Tel: 202-898-0089
Email: aaf@aaf.org
http://www.aaf.org

For information on advertising agencies, contact
American Association of Advertising Agencies
405 Lexington Avenue, 18th Floor
New York, NY 10174-1801
Tel: 212-682-2500
http://www.aaaa.org

For career resources and job listings, contact
American Marketing Association
311 South Wacker Drive, Suite 5800
Chicago, IL 60606-6629
Tel: 800-262-1150

Email: info@ama.org
http://www.marketingpower.com

For information on graduate programs in marketing, contact
Council of American Survey Research Organizations
170 North Country Road, Suite 4
Port Jefferson, NY 11777-2606
Tel: 631-928-6954
Email: casro@casro.org
http://www.casro.org

For information on education and training, contact
Marketing Research Association
110 National Drive, 2nd Floor
Glastonbury, CT 06033-1212
Tel: 860-682-1000
Email: email@mra-net.org
http://www.mra-net.org

Media Planners and Buyers

OVERVIEW

Media specialists are responsible for placing advertisements that will reach targeted customers and get the best response from the market for the least amount of money. Within the media department, *media planners* gather information about the sizes and types of audiences that can be reached through each of the various media and about the cost of advertising in each medium. *Media buyers,* sometimes called *advertising sales agents,* purchase space in printed publications, as well as time on radio or television stations. Advertising media workers are supervised by a *media director,* who is accountable for the overall media plan. In addition to advertising agencies, media planners and buyers work for large companies that purchase space or broadcast time. There are approximately 154,000 advertising sales agents employed in the United States.

HISTORY

The first formal media that allowed advertisers to deliver messages about their products or services to the public were newspapers and magazines, which began selling space to advertisers in the late 19th century. This system of placing ads gave rise to the first media planners and buyers, who were in charge of deciding what kind of advertising to put in which publications and then actually purchasing the space.

In the broadcast realm, radio stations started offering program time to advertisers in the early 1900s. And, while television advertising began just before the end of World War II, producers were quick to realize that they could reach huge audiences by placing ads on TV. Television advertising proved to be beneficial to the TV stations as well, since they relied on sponsors for financial assistance in order to bring programs into people's homes. In the past, programs were sometimes named not for the host or star of the program, but for the sponsoring company that was paying for the broadcast of that particular show.

During the early years of radio and television, it was often possible for one sponsor to pay for an entire 30-minute program. The cost of producing shows on radio and television, however, increased dramatically, requiring many sponsors to support a single radio or television program. Media planners and buyers learned to get more for their money by buying smaller amounts of time—60-, 30-, and even 10-second spots—on a greater number of programs.

Today's media planners and buyers have a wide array of media from which to choose. The newest of these, the World Wide Web, allows advertisers not only to precisely target customers but to interact with them as well. In addition to Web banner ads, producers can also advertise via sponsorships, their own Web sites, CD catalogs, voice-mail telephone shopping, and more. With so many choices, media planners and buyers must carefully determine target markets and select the ideal media mix in order to reach these markets at the least cost.

THE JOB

While many employees may work in the media department, the primary specialists are the media planner and the media buyer. They work with professionals from a wide range of media—from billboards, direct mail, and newspapers and magazines to television, radio, and the Internet. Both types of media specialists must be familiar with the markets that each medium reaches, as well as the advantages and disadvantages of advertising in each.

Media planners determine target markets based on their clients' advertising approaches. Considering their clients' products and services, budget, and image, media planners gather information about the public's viewing, reading, and buying habits by administering questionnaires and conducting other forms of market research. Through this research, planners are able to identify target markets by sorting data according to people's ages, incomes, marital status, interests, and leisure activities.

By knowing which groups of people watch certain shows, listen to specific radio stations, or read particular magazines or newspapers, media planners can help clients select air time or print space to reach the consumers most likely to buy their products.

Media planners try to land contracts by inviting clients to meetings and presentations and educating them about various marketing strategies. They must not only pursue new clients but also attend to current ones, making sure that they are happy with their existing advertising packages. For both new and existing clients, the media planner's main objective is to sell as much air time or ad space as possible.

Media buyers do the actual purchasing of the time on radio or television or the space in a newspaper or magazine in which an advertisement will run. In addition to tracking the time and space available for purchase, media buyers ensure that ads appear when and where they should, negotiate costs for ad placement, and calculate rates, usage, and budgets. They are also responsible for maintaining contact with clients, keeping them informed of all advertising-related developments and resolving any conflicts that arise. Large companies that generate a lot of advertising or those that place only print ads or only broadcast ads sometimes differentiate between the two main media groups by employing *space buyers* and/or *time buyers*.

Workers who actually sell the print space or air time to advertisers are called *print sales workers* or *broadcast time salespeople*. Like media planners, these professionals are well versed about the target markets served by their organizations and can often provide useful information about editorial content or broadcast programs.

In contrast to print and broadcast planners and buyers, *interactive media specialists* are responsible for managing all critical aspects of their clients' online advertising campaigns. While interactive media planners may have responsibilities similar to those of print or broadcast planners, they also act as new technology specialists, placing and tracking all online ads and maintaining relationships with clients and Webmasters alike.

The typical online media planning process begins with an agency spreadsheet that details the criteria about the media buy. These criteria often include target demographics, start and end dates for the ad campaign, and online objectives. After sending all relevant information to a variety of Web sites, the media specialist receives cost, market, and other data from the sites. Finally, the media specialist places the order and sends all creative information needed to the selected Web sites. Once the order has been placed, the media specialist receives tracking and performance data and then compiles and analyzes the information in preparation for future ad campaigns.

Media planners and buyers may have a wide variety of clients. Magazine and newspaper publishers, film studios, television networks, restaurants, hotel chains, beverage companies, food product manufac-turers, and automobile dealers all need to advertise to attract potential customers. While huge companies, such as motion picture studios, soft drink manufacturers, major airlines, and vacation resorts, pay a lot of money to have their products or services advertised nation-ally, many smaller firms need to advertise only in their immediate area. Local advertising may come from a health club that wants to announce a special membership rate or from a retail store promoting a sale. Media planners and buyers must be aware of their various clients' advertising needs and create campaigns that will accomplish their promotional objectives.

REQUIREMENTS

High School

Although most media positions, including those at the entry level, require a bachelor's degree, you can prepare for a future job as media planner and/or buyer by taking specific courses offered at the high school level. These include business, marketing, advertising, cinematography, radio and television, and film and video. General liberal arts classes, such as economics, English, communication, and journalism, are also important, since media planners and buyers must be able to communicate clearly with both clients and cowork-ers. In addition, mathematics classes will give you the skills to work accurately with budget figures and placement costs.

Postsecondary Training

Increasingly, media planners and buyers have college degrees, often with majors in marketing or advertising. Even if you have prior work experience or training in media, you should select college classes that provide a good balance of business course work, broadcast and print experience, and liberal arts studies.

Business classes may include economics, marketing, sales, and advertising. In addition, courses that focus on specific media, such as cinematography, film and video, radio and television, and new technologies (like the Internet), are important. Additional classes in journalism, English, and speech will prove helpful as well. Media directors often need to have a master's degree, as well as extensive experience working with the various media.

Other Requirements

Media planners and buyers in broadcasting should have a keen understanding of programming and consumer buying trends, as well as a knowledge of each potential client's business. Print media specialists must be familiar with the process involved in creating print ads and the markets reached by various publications. In addition, all media workers need to be capable of maintaining good relationships with current clients, as well as pursuing new clients on a continual basis.

Communication and problem solving skills are important, as are creativity, common sense, patience, and persistence. Media planners and buyers must also have excellent oral, written, and analytical skills, knowledge of interactive media planning trends and tools, and the ability to handle multiple assignments in a fast-paced work environment. Strategic thinking skills, industry interest, and computer experience with both database and word processing programs are also vital.

EXPLORING

Many high schools and two-year colleges and most four-year colleges have media departments that may include radio stations and public access or cable television channels. In order to gain worthwhile experience in media, you can work for these departments as aides, production assistants, programmers, or writers. In addition, high school and college newspapers and yearbooks often need students to sell advertising to local merchants. Theater departments also frequently look for people to sell ads for performance programs.

In the local community, newspapers and other publications often hire high school students to work part time and/or in the summer in sales and clerical positions for the classified advertising department. Some towns have cable television stations that regularly look for volunteers to operate cameras, sell advertising, and coordinate various programs. In addition, a variety of religious-sponsored activities, such as craft fairs, holiday boutiques, and rummage sales, can provide you with opportunities to create and place ads and work with the local media in order to get exposure for the events.

EMPLOYERS

Media planners and buyers often work for advertising agencies in large cities, such as Chicago, New York, and Los Angeles. These agencies represent various clients who are trying to sell everything from newspaper and magazine subscriptions to dishwasher soap to the latest comedy featuring the hot star of the moment. Other media specialists work directly for radio and television networks, newspapers, magazines, and Web sites selling airtime and print space. While many of these media organizations are located in large urban areas, particularly radio and television stations, most small towns put out newspapers and therefore need specialists to sell ad space and coordinate accounts. Approximately 154,000 advertising sales agents work in the United States. More than 30 percent of agents work in newspaper, book, and directory publishing.

STARTING OUT

More than half of the jobs in print and broadcast media do not remain open long enough for companies to advertise available positions in the classified sections of newspapers. As a result, many media organizations, such as radio and television stations, do not usually advertise job openings in the want ads. Media planners and buyers often hear about available positions through friends, acquaintances, or family members and frequently enter the field as entry-level broadcasting or sales associates. Both broadcasting and sales can provide employees just starting out with experience in approaching and working for clients, as well as knowledge about the specifics of programming and its relation to selling air time.

Advertising agencies sometimes do advertise job openings, both in local and national papers and on the Web. Competition is quite fierce for entry-level jobs, however, particularly at large agencies in big cities.

Print media employees often start working on smaller publications as in-house sales staff members, answering telephones and taking orders from customers. Other duties may include handling classified ads or coordinating the production and placement of small print ads created by in-house artists. While publications often advertise for entry-level positions, the best way to find work in advertising is to send resumes to as many agencies, publications, and broadcasting offices as possible. With any luck, your resume will arrive just as an opening is becoming available.

While you are enrolled in a college program, you should investigate opportunities for internships or on-campus employment in related areas. Your school's career planning center or placement office should have information on such positions. Previous experience often provides a competitive edge for all job seekers, but it is crucial to aspiring media planners and buyers.

ADVANCEMENT

Large agencies and networks often hire only experienced people, so it is common for media planners and buyers to learn the business at smaller companies. These opportunities allow media specialists to gain the experience and confidence they need to move up to more advanced positions. Jobs at smaller agencies and television and radio stations also provide possibilities for more rapid promotion than those at larger organizations.

Media planners and buyers climbing the company ladder can advance to the position of media director or may earn promotions to executive-level positions. For those already at the management level, advancement can come in the form of larger clients and more responsibility. In addition, many media planners and buyers who have experience with traditional media are investigating the opportunities and challenges that come with the job of *interactive media planner/buyer* or *Web media specialist.*

EARNINGS

Because media planners and buyers work for a variety of organizations all across the country and abroad, earnings can vary greatly. Media directors can earn between $46,000 and $118,400, depending on the type of employer and the director's experience level. For example, directors at small agencies make an average of $42,100, while those at large agencies can earn more than $120,000, according to a 2002 *Advertising Age* salary survey.

Media planners and buyers in television typically earn higher salaries than those in radio. In general, however, beginning broadcasting salespeople usually earn between $18,000 and $35,000 per year and can advance to as much as $46,000 after a few years of experience.

According to the U.S. Department of Labor, advertising sales agents had salaries that ranged from less than $21,080 to more than $89,710 in 2005. Advertising sales agents employed in newspaper, book, and directory publishing had mean annual earnings of $43,910 in 2005.

Most employers of media planners and buyers offer a variety of benefits, including health and life insurance, a retirement plan, and paid vacation and sick days.

WORK ENVIRONMENT

Although media planners and buyers often work a 40-hour week, their hours are not strictly nine to five. Service calls, presentations, and meetings with ad space reps and clients are important parts of the job that usually have a profound effect on work schedules. In addition, media planners and buyers must invest considerable time

Top 10 U.S. Newspapers by Circulation, 2006

Newspaper	Circulation	Web Site
1. USA Today	2,528,437	http://www.usatoday.com
2. The Wall Street Journal	2,058,342	http://online.wsj.com/public/us
3. The New York Times	1,683,855	http://www.nytimes.com
4. Los Angeles Times	1,231,318	http://www.latimes.com
5. The Washington Post	960,684	http://www.washingtonpost.com
6. Chicago Tribune	957,212	http://www.chicagotribune.com
7. New York Daily News	795,153	http://www.nydailynews.com
8. The Philadelphia Inquirer	705,965	http://www.philly.com/mld/inquirer
9. Denver Post/Rocky Mountain News	704,806	http://www.denverpost.com and http://www.rockymountainnews.com
10. Houston Chronicle	692,557	http://www.chron.com

Source: Audit Bureau of Circulations

investigating and reading about trends in programming, buying, and advertising.

The variety of opportunities for media planners and buyers results in a wide diversity of working conditions. Larger advertising agencies, publications, and networks may have modern and comfortable working facilities. Smaller markets may have more modest working environments.

Whatever the size of the organization, many planners seldom go into the office and must call in to keep in touch with the home organization. Travel is a big part of media planners' responsibilities to their clients, and they may have clients in many different types of businesses and services, as well as in different areas of the country.

While much of the media planner and buyer's job requires interaction with a variety of people, including coworkers, sales reps, supervisors, and clients, most media specialists also perform many tasks that require independent work, such as researching and writing reports. In any case, the media planner and buyer must be able to handle many tasks at the same time in a fast-paced, continually changing environment.

OUTLOOK

The employment outlook for media planners and buyers, like the outlook for the advertising industry itself, depends on the general health of the economy. When the economy thrives, companies produce an increasing number of goods and seek to promote them via newspapers, magazines, television, radio, the Internet, and various other media. The U.S. Department of Labor anticipates that employment in the advertising industry is projected to grow 22 percent over the 2004-14 period. This is faster than the average for all industries.

More and more people are relying on radio and television for their entertainment and information. With cable and local television channels offering a wide variety of programs, advertisers are increasingly turning to TV in order to get exposure for their products and services. Although newspaper sales are in decline, there is growth in special interest periodicals and other print publications. Interactive media, such as the Internet, CD catalogs, and voice-mail shopping, are providing a flurry of advertising activity all around the world. All of this activity will increase market opportunities for media planners and buyers.

Employment possibilities for media specialists are far greater in large cities, such as New York, Los Angeles, and Chicago, where most magazines and many broadcast networks have their headquarters. However, smaller publications are often located in outlying areas, and large national organizations usually have sales offices in several cities across the country.

Competition for all advertising positions, including entry-level jobs, is expected to be intense. Media planners and buyers who have considerable experience will have the best chances of finding employment.

FOR MORE INFORMATION

For information on college chapters, internship opportunities, and financial aid opportunities, contact
American Advertising Federation
1101 Vermont Avenue, NW, Suite 500
Washington, DC 20005-6306
Tel: 202-898-0089

Email: aaf@aaf.org
http://www.aaf.org

For information on advertising agencies, contact
American Association of Advertising Agencies
405 Lexington Avenue, 18th Floor
New York, NY 10174-1801
Tel: 212-682-2500
http://www.aaaa.org

For career resources and job listings, contact
American Marketing Association
311 South Wacker Drive, Suite 5800
Chicago, IL 60606-6629
Tel: 800-262-1150
Email: info@ama.org
http://www.marketingpower.com

For information on education and training, contact
Marketing Research Association
110 National Drive, 2nd Floor
Glastonbury, CT 06033-1212
Tel: 860-682-1000
Email: email@mra-net.org
http://www.mra-net.org

Newspaper Editors

OVERVIEW

Newspaper editors assign, review, edit, rewrite, and lay out all copy in a newspaper except advertisements. Editors sometimes write stories or editorials that offer opinions on issues. Editors review the editorial page and copy written by staff or syndicated columnists. A large metropolitan daily newspaper staff may include various editors who process thousands of words into print daily. A small-town staff of a weekly newspaper, however, may include only one editor, who might be both owner and star reporter. Large metropolitan areas, such as New York, Los Angeles, Chicago, and Washington, D.C., employ many editors. Approximately 127,000 editors work for publications of all types in the United States.

HISTORY

Journalism may have begun in Rome with the regular publication of reports called *Acta Diurna,* or "Daily Acts," begun in 59 B.C. They reported political news and social events on a daily basis. In China, a journal called the *pao* was published on a regular basis from A.D. 618 until 1911, recording activities of the court. The first regularly printed European newspapers appeared in the early 1700s in Germany, The Netherlands, and Italy. The Dutch *corantos,* composed of items from the foreign press, were translated into English and French around 1620. The first English newspaper is considered to be the *Weekly Newes,* initially published in 1622. Until 1644, the news in English journals was controlled by the Star Chamber, a court that censored any unfavorable information about the king. Interestingly, also in 1644, the chamber was dismissed, and the English enjoyed the first semblance of freedom of the press. It was not until 1670 that the term "newspaper" came into use.

QUICK FACTS

School Subjects
English
Journalism

Personal Interests
Communication/ideas
Helping/teaching

Work Environment
Primarily indoors
Primarily one location

Minimum Education Level
Bachelor's degree

Salary Range
$26,910 to $51,030 to
$85,230+

Certification or Licensing
None available

Outlook
About as fast as the average

DOT
132

GOE
11.08.01

NOC
5122

O*NET-SOC
27-3041.00

Benjamin Harris, an English journalist who emigrated to the United States, published the first American colonial newspaper in Boston in 1690, but because of the repressive climate of the times, it was immediately closed down by the British governor.

The first regularly circulated newspaper in the colonies was the *Boston News-Letter,* a weekly first published in 1704 by John Campbell. The press at this time still operated under rather severe government restrictions, but the struggle for freedom of the press grew, and before the end of the century, journalists were able to print the news without fear of repression.

The need for newspaper editors grew rapidly through the 19th and early 20th centuries as the demand for newspapers grew, causing circulation to jump from thousands to millions. New technology allowed the newspaper industry to meet the demand. Presses were invented that could produce newspapers by the millions on a daily basis.

In the 19th century, newspaper publishers began to endorse political candidates and to take stands on other political and social issues. They also came to be sources of entertainment. When Benjamin Day founded the *New York Sun* in 1833, he sought to do more than inform. The paper's pages were filled with news from the police beat as well as gossip, disasters, animal stories, and anecdotes. Other papers of the era began to print sports news, particularly horse racing and prize fights, society pages, and the business news from Wall Street. By the mid-19th century, there was an outpouring of human interest news, and journalists discovered the public appetite for scandal. By the end of the century, a number of newspaper editors were famed for their craft, including Horace Greeley of the *New York Tribune,* Charles A. Dana of the *New York Sun,* and William Allen White of the *Kansas Gazette.*

Newspaper sensationalism reached its peak during the last years of the 19th century and the first decades of the 20th. The most notable figure in this period of "yellow journalism" was William Randolph Hearst. He built a vast newspaper empire by playing on the emotions of his readership. Hearst often fabricated news, as did others, including his chief rival of the period, Joseph Pulitzer of the *New York World.* Perhaps the most glaring example of this type of journalism was Hearst and Pulitzer's exaggerated treatment of Spanish atrocities in Cuba, which incited public sentiment for war against Spain. Historians feel that the news coverage was at least partially responsible for the declaration of war that came in 1898. Although most newspapers through the 20th century have adhered to ethical journalistic practices, a number of dailies and weekly tabloids, protected by freedom of the press, continue to exploit the

Editors at the *Post-Standard* (Syracuse) participate in a budget meeting in the newsroom. *(The Image Works)*

sensationalist market. Journalists in general, however, have adopted codes, such as that of the Society of Professional Journalists, which stress responsibility, freedom of the press, ethics, accuracy, objectivity, and fair play.

By the 20th century, newspapers became big business. Many newspaper publishing companies became corporate conglomerates that owned printing plants, radio and television stations, paper plants, forest acreage, and other related assets. Most of the profits came from advertising dollars as newspapers became the leading medium for advertising. As costs rose, it took more and more advertising to support the news portion of the paper, until advertising occupied most of the space in almost all U.S. newspapers. The amount of advertising, in most cases, now determines the amount of news coverage a newspaper carries. Eventually, many newspapers could not withstand the rising costs and the increased competition from television. From the mid-20th century newspapers started declining at a rapid rate. Between 1950 and 2005, for instance, the number of daily papers in the United States fell from 1,772 to 1,452.

As some papers failed, others, especially in large cities, grew as they took over new circulation. The major metropolitan dailies continued to add new and more exciting features in order to keep up with the competition, especially television.

From the beginning of the century, newspapers had been expanding their coverage, and on large papers, editorial departments came to be divided into many specialty areas, requiring reporters and editors with equivalent specialties. Today, most newspapers have departments devoted to entertainment, sports, business, science, consumer affairs, education, and just about every other area of interest in today's society. Many also have online version which feature articles from print editions as well as Internet exclusives.

THE JOB

Newspaper editors are responsible for the paper's entire news content. The news section includes features, "hard" news, and editorial commentary. Editors of a daily paper plan the contents of each day's issue, assigning articles, reviewing submissions, prioritizing stories, checking wire services, selecting illustrations, and laying out each page with the advertising space allotted.

At a large daily newspaper, an *editor in chief* oversees the entire editorial operation, determines its editorial policy, and reports to the publisher. The *managing editor* is responsible for day-to-day operations in an administrative capacity. *Story editors,* or *wire editors,* determine which national news agency (or wire service) stories will be used and edit them. Wire services give smaller papers, without foreign correspondents, access to international stories.

A *city editor* gathers local and sometimes state and national news. The city editor hires copy editors and reporters, hands out assignments to reporters and photographers, reviews and edits stories, confers with executive editors on story content and space availability, and gives stories to copy editors for final editing.

A newspaper may have separate desks for state, national, and foreign news, each with its own head editor. Some papers have separate *editorial page editors.* The *department editors* oversee individual features; they include *business editors, fashion editors, sports editors, book section editors, entertainment editors,* and more. Department heads make decisions on coverage, recommend story ideas, and make assignments. They often have backgrounds in their department's subject matter and are highly skilled at writing and editing.

The copy desk, the story's last stop, is staffed by *copy editors,* who correct spelling, grammar, and punctuation mistakes; check for readability and sense; edit for clarification; examine stories for factual accuracy; and ensure the story conforms to editorial policy. Copy editors sometimes write headlines or picture captions and may crop photos. Occasionally they find serious problems that cause them to kick stories back to the editors or the writer.

Editors, particularly copy editors, base many of their decisions on a style book that provides preferences in spelling, grammar, and word usage; it indicates when to use foreign spellings or English translations and the preferred system of transliteration. Some houses develop their own style books, but often they use or adapt the *Associated Press Stylebook.*

After editors approve the story's organization, coverage, writing quality, and accuracy, they turn it over to the *news editors,* who supervise article placement and determine page layout with the advertising department. News and executive editors discuss the relative priorities of major news stories. If a paper is divided into several sections, each has its own priorities.

Modern newspaper editors depend heavily on computers. Generally, a reporter types the story directly onto the computer network, providing editors with immediate access. Some editorial departments are situated remotely from printing facilities, but computers allow the printer to receive copy immediately upon approval. Today, designers computerize page layout. Many columnists send their finished columns from home computers to the editorial department via modem.

REQUIREMENTS

High School
English is the most important school subject for any future editor. You must have a strong grasp of the English language, including vocabulary, grammar, and punctuation, and you must be able to write well in various styles. Study journalism and take communications-related courses. Work as a writer or editor for your school paper or yearbook. Computer classes that teach word processing software and how to navigate the Internet will be invaluable in your future research. You absolutely must learn to type. If you cannot type accurately and rapidly, you will be at an extreme disadvantage.

Other subjects are important, too. Editors have knowledge in a wide range of topics, and the more you know about history, geography, math, the sciences, the arts, and culture, the better writer and editor you will be.

Postsecondary Training
Look for a school with strong journalism and communications programs. Many programs require you to complete two years of liberal arts studies before concentrating on journalism studies. Journalism courses include reporting, writing, and editing; press law and ethics; journalism history; and photojournalism. Advanced classes include feature writing, investigative reporting, and graphics. Some schools offer internships for credit.

When hiring, newspapers look closely at a candidate's extracurricular activities, putting special emphasis on internships, school newspaper and freelance writing and editing, and part-time newspaper work (stringing). Typing, computer skills, and knowledge of printing are helpful.

Other Requirements

To be a successful newspaper editor, you must have a love of learning, reading, and writing. You should enjoy the process of discovering information and presenting it to a wide audience in a complete, precise, and understandable way. You must be detail-oriented and care about the finer points of accuracy, not only in writing, but in reporting and presentation. You must be able to work well with coworkers, both giving and taking direction, and you must be able to work alone. Editors can spend long hours sitting at a desk in front of a computer screen.

EXPLORING

One of the best ways to explore this job is by working on your school's newspaper or other publication. You will most probably start as a staff writer or proofreader, but the experience will help you understand editing and how it relates to the entire field of publishing.

Keeping a journal is another good way to polish your writing skills and explore your interest in writing and editing your own work. In fact, any writing project will be helpful, since editing and writing are inextricably linked. Make an effort to write every day, even if it is only a few paragraphs. Try different kinds of writing, such as letters to the editor, short stories, poetry, essays, comedic prose, and plays.

EMPLOYERS

There are approximately 127,000 editors in the United States. Generally, newspaper editors are employed in every city or town, as most towns have at least one newspaper. As the population multiplies, so do the opportunities. In large metropolitan areas, there may be one or two daily papers, several general interest weekly papers, ethnic and other special-interest newspapers, trade newspapers, and daily and weekly community and suburban newspapers. All of these publications need managing and department editors. Online papers also provide opportunities for editors.

STARTING OUT

A typical route of entry into this field is by working as an editorial assistant or proofreader. Editorial assistants perform clerical tasks as well as some proofreading and other basic editorial tasks. Proofreaders can learn about editorial jobs while they work on a piece by looking at editors' comments on their work.

Job openings can be found using school career services offices, classified ads in newspapers and trade journals, and specialized publications such as *Publishers Weekly* (http://www.publishersweekly.com). In addition, many publishers have Web sites that list job openings, and large publishers often have telephone job lines that serve the same purpose.

ADVANCEMENT

Newspaper editors generally begin working on the copy desk, where they progress from less significant stories and projects to major news and feature stories. A common route to advancement is for copy editors to be promoted to a particular department, where they may move up the ranks to management positions. An editor who has achieved success in a department may become a city editor, who is responsible for news, or a managing editor, who runs the entire editorial operation of a newspaper.

EARNINGS

Salaries for newspaper editors vary from small to large communities, but editors generally are well compensated. Other factors affecting compensation include quality of education and previous experience, job level, and the newspaper's circulation. Large metropolitan dailies offer higher-paying jobs, while outlying weekly papers pay less.

According to the U.S. Department of Labor, the mean annual income for newspaper, periodical, book, and directory publishers editors was $51,030 in 2005. Salaries for all editors ranged from less than $26,910 to more than $85,230 annually.

On many newspapers, salary ranges and benefits, such as vacation time and health insurance, for most nonmanagerial editorial workers are negotiated by The Newspaper Guild.

WORK ENVIRONMENT

The environments in which editors work vary widely. For the most part, publishers of all kinds realize that a quiet atmosphere is conducive to work that requires tremendous concentration. It takes an unusual ability to edit in a noisy place. Most editors work in private offices or cubicles. Even in relatively quiet surroundings, however, editors often have many distractions. In many cases, editors have computers that are exclusively for their own use, but in others, editors must share computers that are located in a common area.

Deadlines are an important issue for virtually all editors. Newspaper editors work in a much more pressured atmosphere than other editors because they face daily or weekly deadlines. To meet these deadlines, newspaper editors often work long hours. Some newspaper editors start work at 5 A.M., others work until 11 P.M. or even through the night. Those who work on weekly newspapers, including feature editors, columnists, and editorial page editors, usually work more regular hours.

OUTLOOK

According to the U.S. Department of Labor, employment for editors and writers, while highly competitive, should grow about as fast as the average for all occupations through 2014. Opportunities will be better on small daily and weekly newspapers, where the pay is lower. Some publications hire freelance editors to support reduced full-time staffs. And as experienced editors leave the workforce or move to other fields, job openings will occur.

FOR MORE INFORMATION

The ASNE helps editors maintain the highest standards of quality, improve their craft, and better serve their communities. It preserves and promotes core journalistic values. Visit its Web site to read online publications such as Why Choose Journalism? *and* Preparing for a Career in Newspapers.

American Society of Newspaper Editors (ASNE)
11690B Sunrise Valley Drive
Reston, VA 20191-1409
Tel: 703-453-1122
Email: asne@asne.org
http://www.asne.org

Founded in 1958 by The Wall Street Journal *to improve the quality of journalism education, this organization offers internships, scholarships, and literature for college students. To read* The Journalist's Road to Success: A Career Guide, *which lists schools offering degrees in news-editing, and financial aid to those interested in print journalism, visit the DJNF's Web site.*

Dow Jones Newspaper Fund (DJNF)
PO Box 300
Princeton, NJ 08543-0300
Tel: 609-452-2820
Email: newsfund@wsj.dowjones.com
http://djnewspaperfund.dowjones.com

This trade association for African-American-owned newspapers has a foundation that offers a scholarship and internship program for inner-city high school juniors.

National Newspaper Publishers Association
3200 13th Street, NW
Washington, DC 20010-2410
Tel: 202-588-8764
Email: nnpa@nnpa.org
http://www.nnpa.org

For information on the newspaper industry, contact
Newspaper Association of America
4401 Wilson Boulevard, Suite 900
Arlington, VA 22203-1867
Tel: 571-366-1000
Email: IRC@naa.org
http://www.naa.org

This organization for journalists has campus and online chapters.
Society of Professional Journalists
Eugene S. Pulliam National Journalism Center
3909 North Meridian Street
Indianapolis, IN 46208-4011
Tel: 317-927-8000
http://www.spj.org

Visit the following Web site for comprehensive information on journalism careers, summer programs, and college journalism programs.
High School Journalism
http://www.highschooljournalism.org

Online Producers

OVERVIEW

Online producers are responsible for organizing and presenting information that is available on Web sites. They edit and/or write news stories, arrange the text, and any accompanying photos for online publication. They sometimes work with other workers to incorporate slideshows, background music, or audio interviews to better complement a story. While many online producers are employed in journalism, a growing number of producers find work managing corporate Web sites for advertising agencies, employment firms, pharmaceutical companies, nonprofits, and other organizations. Online producers are also referred to as *content producers* and *online editors*.

HISTORY

The manner in which people receive news and other information has changed with the popularity of computers and access to the Internet. People crave news—from breaking stories to real-time baseball scores—and are no longer willing to wait until the next morning's edition of their favorite newspaper to stay up to speed with the world around them. Also, portable computers and PDAs have made access to the Internet possible while commuting to and from work. Web-based editions of newspapers, television stations, magazines, and radio stations have quickly found an audience. Online producers, professionals with writing and editing skills, as well as computer savvy, are needed to maintain these sites with well written and presented articles. Additionally, online producers are in demand in non-journalistic settings as many businesses and other organizations seek a place on the Internet.

THE JOB

Online producers working in journalism are responsible for the daily writing/editing and presentation of information appearing on their organization's Web sites. Most forms of media—newspapers, magazines, television, and radio—have a web-based equivalent where people can access news and information on a 24-hour basis. Online producers take news articles originally published in that day's paper or broadcast, and translate them into appropriate content for the organization's Web site. If new developments have occurred since the story was first printed, they are incorporated into the online version. Special coding is added to the article, most often HTML, which allows the text to be posted on a Web site. Links or related keywords are added so the article will show up in searches and archives.

The web version of a story must be presented in a different way then it is on paper—text is often edited to be more concise and engaging to the reader. The layout of the entire article is key—if it doesn't grab the reader's attention, the story may be ignored by online readers. Online producers may choose to include features such as photos, video, animation, music, or art. Since space is not an issue on the Web, many articles run with sidebars, photos, and other features not originally included in the print or broadcast edition. Online producers often work with multimedia producers to create special content packages such as videos or an audio slide show—a series of photos presented with an audio voiceover—to further enhance a story. Other stories lend themselves to special art provided by different vendors. Online producers, working with the advertising and technical departments, decide on which pieces to purchase and use. Sports sections, for example, oftentimes use team rosters and statistics to complement special event coverage such as the Super Bowl, the World Series, or the Olympic Games.

On an average shift, online producers can expect to produce about two to four dozen stories. Many of the stories are filtered from the day's print edition, but some will be reported directly from the field, or from newswire services. Some online producers, especially at smaller companies, are responsible for producing all news stories, regardless of subject. Online producers employed at large media companies may be assigned a specific beat or area of expertise such as world news or sports. Teamwork is part of the job as well. When an important story unfolds or a special edition is being created to cover a major event--such as the death of a religious leader or a presidential election--online producers will work with other members of the editorial staff to get the news posted as quickly as possible.

REQUIREMENTS

High School

Solid computer skills will give you the edge over other candidates. Prepare yourself by enrolling in every computer class your school has to offer, from programming to Web site design. Familiarize yourself with different software programs such as Adobe Photoshop, Macromedia DreamWeaver, or Macromedia HomeSite and different markup languages such as HTML. Round out your education with classes such as business, math, and English. Since many online producers have a journalism background, you'll need strong reporting, writing, and editing skills to keep up with the competition. Any classes that require written reports as regular assignments are wise choices.

Postsecondary Training

While there are many routes of study in preparation for this career, many online producers enter the field after earning a bachelor's degree in journalism. In fact, many schools now offer web-based media classes as an elective to their traditional journalism studies. Northwestern University's Medill School of Journalism, for example, now offers a New Media concentration alongside traditional print, broadcast, and magazine journalism curricula at the undergraduate and graduate level. Besides the demands of good reporting and writing, New Media students are taught various computer languages, publishing software, and interactive tools needed to present news online, as well as how to address the challenges of instant, space unlimited publishing. Check out Medill's Web site (http://www.medill.northwestern.edu/journalism/newmedia/index.html) for more information.

Other Requirements

Do you perform well under pressure? Can you quickly change gears and focus on a completely different project without complaining or losing momentum? Are you self-motivated and an independent worker, yet capable of being a team player? If you answer yes to these questions, you have some of the skills that are necessary for success in this industry.

EXPLORING

Creating your own Web site is an excellent way to explore this career. Not only will you gain experience in Web design, coding, and different software programs, you'll have total editorial control.

Does your school paper have a Web site? If not, take the initiative and build one. As online producer for this project, you can add photo slideshows of the school prom, add a team roster graphic for the winning basketball team, and spice up your site with links to school clubs and organizations.

You should also surf the web to view existing news and corporate Web sites. Write down what you like and dislike about each. Are the links relevant? Is the story portrayed in a concise, yet informative manner? If given the chance, what improvements would you make?

You might also consider becoming a student member of the Online News Association, a professional organization for online journalism professionals. Besides presenting the latest industry news, the association's Web site offers a wealth of information on available internships, school programs, conferences, and forums. Log onto http://journalist.org/about/archives/000128.php for more information regarding membership at the student level.

STARTING OUT

A job as an assistant or associate online producer is a common starting point for this career. Many companies hiring online producers require at least three years experience in Web journalism. Internships are your best bet to gain experience and training as well as valuable industry contacts for the future.

Check with you school's career counselor for possible leads on summer internships; some publications or companies may hire high school students. Even if you spend your working day running for coffee or answering phones, at least you'll be in the company of industry professionals. Contact your local newspaper to see if any part-time employment opportunities are available during the school year or summer vacation.

Also, check with associations for job leads. The Online News Association posts job openings nationwide. PoynterOnline (http://www.poynter.org/default.asp), besides being a great resource of industry news, offers seminars, fellowships, tip sheets, and links to employment possibilities.

ADVANCEMENT

Larger publications promote experienced online producers to senior or executive status. Those employed at regional publications could seek jobs at larger publications with broader news coverage.

EARNINGS

Although no specific salary statistics are available for online producers, earnings for these professionals are generally similar to that of traditional editors--although online editors may earn slightly more than their print counterparts. According to the U.S. Department of Labor, the median yearly income of traditional editors was $45,510 in 2005. The lowest 10 percent of all editors earned less than $26,910; the highest 10 percent earned more than $85,230. Online producers typically receive benefits such as vacation and sick days and health insurance.

WORK ENVIRONMENT

Online producers--especially those in journalism--work in hectic, fast paced environments. Deadlines are short and may come at any time of the day or night. Online producers must be able to drop a current project, shift gears, and quickly focus on a breaking story. Most online producers have more editorial control as opposed to editors on the print side of a publication. Since much of their work is done after editorial offices have closed for the day, they oftentimes make key decisions on what stories are posted at the organization's Web site.

Web sites operate 24-hours a day, seven days a week. News is often posted minutes after it has occurred. Work shifts are scheduled to accommodate this, and may vary from week to week. Nontraditional work hours can be physically exhausting and, at times, affect an online producer's personal life.

OUTLOOK

The Web has already had a major impact on how people receive and access their news and information. And with the popularity of portable computers and cell phones, and PDAs with Internet access, the number of people turning to web-based news and information is expected to grow. Most, if not all, forms of traditional media—newspapers, magazines, and television—have a web-based counterpart. And with more corporate, small business, and professional organizations seeking a presence on the Web, the need for capable online producers is certain to increase.

Industry experts predict that some duties of online producers, such as story production and layout, may be eventually automated, leaving producers more time for original reporting in the field. Also, look for online producers to enjoy increasing opportunities with startup online publications that do not have ties to a print or broad-cast entity.

FOR MORE INFORMATION

For information on its New Media program, contact
Medill School of Journalism
Northwestern University
1845 Sheridan Road
Evanston, IL 60208-2101
Tel: 847-467-1882
Email: medill-admis@northwestern.edu
http://www.medill.northwestern.edu/journalism/newmedia/
   index.html

For information on internships, school programs, and member-ships, contact
Online News Association
PO Box 2002, Radio City Station
New York, NY 10101-2022
Tel: 646-290-7900
http://www.onlinenewsassociation.org

For information on fellowships, seminars, and employment oppor-tunities, visit
Poynter Online
http://www.poynter.org/default.asp

Photo Editors

OVERVIEW

Photo editors are responsible for the look of final photographs to be published in a book or periodical or that are posted on the Internet. They make photo assignments, judge and alter pictures to meet assignment needs, and make sure all deadlines are met. They work for publishers, advertising agencies, photo stock agencies, greeting card companies, and any employer that relies heavily on visual images to sell its products or services.

HISTORY

For as long as photos have been in print, photo editors have been needed to evaluate them and delegate shooting assignments. In the early days of photography (the late 1800s), the jobs of photographer and editor were generally combined. On the staffs of early newspapers, it was not uncommon to have a story editor evaluate and place photos, or for a reporter to shoot his or her own accompanying photos as well as edit them for print. However, the need for a separate photo editor has become apparent as visual elements have become a larger part of print and online publications, advertisements, and even political campaigns. The trained eye and technical know-how of a photo editor is now an essential part of newsroom staffs and corporate offices everywhere.

QUICK FACTS

School Subjects
Art
Computer science

Personal Skills
Artistic
Communication/ideas

Work Environment
Primarily indoors
Primarily one location

Minimum Education Level
Some postsecondary training

Salary Range
$43,048 to $74,721 to
$74,721+

Certification or licensing
None available

Outlook
About as fast as the average

DOT
143

GOE
01.02.03

NOC
5221

O*NET-SOC
27-4021.00, 27-4021.01,
27-4021.02

THE JOB

The final look of a print or online publication is the result of many workers. The photo editor is responsible for the pictures you see in these publications. They work with photographers, reporters,

A photo editor reviews negatives in her office. (*The Image Works*)

authors, copy editors, and company executives to make sure final photos help to illustrate, enlighten, or inspire the reader.

Photo editors, though knowledgeable in photography, generally leave the shooting to staff or contract photographers. Editors meet with their managers or clients to determine the needs of the project and brainstorm ideas for photos that will meet the project's goals. After picture ideas have been discussed, editors give photographers assignments, always including a firm deadline for completion. Most editors work for companies that face firm deadlines; if the editor doesn't have pictures to work with in time, the whole project is held up.

Once photos have arrived, the editor gets to work, using computer software to crop or enlarge shots, alter the coloring of images, or emphasize the photographer's use of shadows or light. All this work requires knowledge of photography, an aesthetic eye, and an awareness of the project's needs. Editors working for a newspaper must be sure to print photos that are true to life, while editors working for a fine-arts publication can alter images to create a more abstract effect.

Photo editors also use photo stock agencies to meet project needs. Depending on the size and type of company the editor works for, he or she might not have a staff of photographers to work with. Stock agencies fill this need. Editors can browse stock photos for sale online or in brochures. Even with purchased photos, the editor still has to make sure the image fits the needs and space of the project.

In addition to working with photos, editors take on managerial tasks, such as assigning deadlines, organizing the office, ordering supplies, training employees, and overseeing the work of others. Along with copy and project editors, the photo editor is in contact with members of upper management or outside clients, and thus he or she is responsible for communicating their needs and desires to other workers.

REQUIREMENTS

High School

In addition to photography classes, take illustration and other art classes to develop an artistic eye and familiarize yourself with other forms of visual aids that are used in publications. Math classes will come in handy, as editors have to exactly measure the size and resolution of photos. To be able to determine what photo will meet the needs of a project, you will have to do a lot of reading, so English and communications classes are useful. Last but certainly not least, computer science classes will be invaluable. As an editor, you will work with computers almost daily and must be comfortable with art, layout, and word processing programs.

Postsecondary Training

While not required, most large and prestigious companies will want editors with a college degree in photography, visual art, or computer science. Employers will also want experience, so be sure to get as much exposure working on a publication as possible while in school. Other options are to go to a community college for a degree program; many offer programs in art or computer science that should be sufficient.

You should also be more than familiar with photo editing software such as Adobe PhotoShop, Apple iPhoto, and Corel Photo-Paint, just to name a few.

Other Requirements

In addition to technical know-how, you should also be adept at working with people and for people. As an editor, you will often be the liaison between the client or upper management and the reporters and photographers working for you. You need to be able to communicate the needs of the project to all those working on it.

EXPLORING

To see if this career might be for you, explore your interests. Get involved with your school yearbook or newspaper. Both of these publications often appoint student photo editors to assist with photo acquisitions and layout. You should also try your hand at photography. To be a knowledgeable and successful editor, you need to know the medium in which you work.

You could also try to speak to a professional photo editor about his or her work. Ask a teacher or your counselor to set up a meeting, and think of questions to ask the editor ahead of time.

EMPLOYERS

Photo editors work for any organization that produces publications or online newsletters or has a Web site with many photos. This includes publishing houses, large corporations, Web site developers, nonprofit organizations, and the government. A large percentage of photo editors also work for stock photo agencies, either as staff photographers or as freelancers.

STARTING OUT

Photo editors often start out as photographers, staff writers, or other lower-level editors. They have to gain experience in their area of work, whether it is magazine publishing or Web site development, to be able to choose the right photos for their projects.

ADVANCEMENT

Photo editors advance by taking on more supervisory responsibility for their department or by working on larger projects for high-end clients. These positions generally command more money and can lead to chief editorial jobs. Freelance editors advance by working for more clients and charging more money for their services.

EARNINGS

Earnings for photo editors will vary depending on where they work. Salary.com reports that in June 2007, the median expected salary for a typical photo editor was approximately $58,240, but ranged from less than $43,048 to more than $74,721. If the editor is employed by a corporation, stock photo agency, or other business, he or she typically will be entitled to health insurance, vacation time, and other benefits. Self-employed editors have to provide their own health and life insurance, but they can make their own schedules.

WORK ENVIRONMENT

Editors typically work in a comfortable office setting, with computers and other tools nearby. Depending on the workplace, the environment can be quiet and slow, or busy with plenty of interruptions. Deadline pressures can make the job of photo editing hectic at times. Tight production schedules may leave editors with little time to acquire photos or contract work out to photographers. Editors may have a quick turnaround time from when completed photos land on their desk to when the publication has to be sent to the printer. However, unless the editor works for a daily paper or weekly magazine, these busy periods are generally accompanied by slower periods with looser schedules. A good photo editor is flexible and able to work under both conditions.

OUTLOOK

Photo editing has been a popular and in-demand field for many years. More and more companies are relying on a Web presence, complete with engaging visuals, to sell their products or services. Photo editors will also always be needed to help create a polished look to a printed publication, selecting just the right photos to deliver the right message to readers.

Though computers have revolutionized the way that photo editors work—bringing their work from paper to screen—they have also caused some problems. Improved software technology now makes it possible for virtually anyone to scan or download an image and alter it to any specifications. However, most professional publications will still hire photo editors with expertise and a trained eye to do this work.

FOR MORE INFORMATION

The NPPA maintains a job bank, provides educational information, and makes insurance available to its members. It also publishes News Photographer *magazine.*

National Press Photographers Association (NPPA)
3200 Croasdaile Drive, Suite 306
Durham, NC 27705-2588
Tel: 919-383-7246
Email: info@nppa.org
http://www.nppa.org

This organization provides training, publishes its own magazine, and offers various services for its members.

Professional Photographers of America
229 Peachtree Street, NE, Suite 2200
Atlanta, GA 30303-1608

Tel: 800-786-6277
Email: csc@ppa.com
http://www.ppa.com

This organization provides workshops, conferences, and other professional meetings for "management or leadership-level people responsible for overseeing photography at their publications." Visit its Web site to read articles on news and developments within the industry.

Associated Press Photo Managers
Email: appm@ap.org
http://www.apphotomanagers.org

Check out this site to see examples of high-quality stock photos.

Stock Solution's Top Photo Site of the Week
http://www.tssphoto.com/foto_week.html

Photographers and Photojournalists

OVERVIEW

Photographers take and sometimes develop and print pictures of people, places, objects, and events, using a variety of cameras and photographic equipment. They work in the publishing, advertising, public relations, science, and business industries, as well as provide personal photographic services. They may also work as fine artists.

Photojournalists shoot photographs that capture news events. Their job is to tell a story with pictures. They may cover a war in central Africa, the Olympics, a national election, or a small-town Fourth of July parade. In addition to shooting pictures, they also write captions or other supporting text to provide further detail about each photograph. Photojournalists may also develop and print photographs or edit film. There are approximately 129,000 photographers and photojournalists employed in the United States.

HISTORY

The word *photograph* means "to write with light." Although the art of photography goes back only about 150 years, the two Greek words that were chosen and combined to refer to this skill quite accurately describe what it does.

The discoveries that led eventually to photography began early in the 18th century when a German scientist, Dr. Johann H. Schultze, experimented with the action of light on certain chemicals. He found that when these chemicals were covered by dark paper they did not change color, but when they were exposed to sunlight, they darkened. A French painter named Louis Daguerre became the first photographer in 1839, using silver-iodide-coated plates and a small box. To develop images on the plates, Daguerre exposed them to mercury vapor. The daguerreotype, as these early photographs came to be known, took minutes to expose and the developing process was directly to the plate. There were no prints made.

Although the daguerreotype was the sensation of its day, it was not until George Eastman invented a simple camera and flexible roll film that photography began to come into widespread use in the late 1800s. After exposing this film to light and developing it with chemicals, the film revealed a color-reversed image, which is called a negative. To make the negative positive (aka: print a picture), light must be shone though the negative onto light-sensitive paper. This process can be repeated to make multiple copies of an image from one negative.

Photojournalism started in the early 1920s with the development of new camera equipment that could be easily transported as news occurred. A growing market for photographically illustrated magazines revealed a population wanting news told through pictures—and also reflected a relatively low level of literacy among the general public. As World Wars I and II ravaged Europe and the rest of the world, reporters were either handed a camera or were accompanied by photographers to capture the gruesome and sometimes inspirational images of courage during combat.

In 1936, *Life* magazine was launched and quickly became one of the most popular vehicles for the photo essay, a news piece consisting mainly of photographs and their accompanying captions. Soon, however, photojournalists left the illustrated magazine market for news organizations catering to the larger newspapers and television networks. Less emphasis was placed on the photo essay; instead, photojournalists were more often asked to track celebrities or gather photos for newspaper advertising.

One of the most important developments in recent years is digital photography. In digital photography, instead of using film, pictures are recorded on microchips, which can then be downloaded onto a computer's hard drive. They can be manipulated in size, color, and shape, virtually eliminating the need for a darkroom.

Digital photography has also affected the field of photojournalism. Many papers have pared down their photography staff and purchase stock photos from photo agencies. Some smaller papers might even hand staff reporters digital cameras to illustrate their own stories. Still, photojournalists have a place in the working world, as their trained "eyes" for perfect shots will always be in demand.

A photojournalist takes a break during the U.S. military's push toward Baghdad, Iraq, during Gulf War II in 2003. *(The Image Works)*

THE JOB

Photography is both an artistic and technical occupation. There are many variables in the process that a knowledgeable photographer can manipulate to produce a clear image or a more abstract work of fine art. First, all photographers (including photojournalists) know how to use cameras and can adjust focus, shutter speeds, aperture, lenses, and filters. They know about the types and speeds of films. Photographers also know about light and shadow, deciding when to use available natural light and when to set up artificial lighting to achieve desired effects.

Some photographers send their film to laboratories, but others develop their own negatives and make their own prints. These processes require knowledge about chemicals such as developers and fixers and how to use enlarging equipment. Photographers must also be familiar with the large variety of papers available for printing photographs, all of which deliver a different effect. Most photographers continually experiment with photographic processes to improve their technical proficiency or to create special effects.

Digital photography is a relatively new development. With this new technology, film is replaced by microchips that record pictures in digital format. Pictures can then be downloaded onto a computer's hard drive. Photographers use special software to manipulate the images on screen.

Photographers usually specialize in one of several areas: portraiture, commercial and advertising photography, fine art, educational photography, or scientific photography. There are subspecialties within each of these categories. A *scientific photographer*, for example, may specialize in aerial or underwater photography. A *commercial photographer* may specialize in food or fashion photography.

Another popular specialty for photographers is photojournalism. Photojournalists are photographers who capture stories of everyday life or news events that, supported with words, tell stories to the entire world or to the smallest of communities. Photojournalists are the eyes of the community, allowing viewers to be a part of events that they would otherwise not have access to.

Actually shooting the photographs is just a portion of what photojournalists do. They also write the cutlines or captions that go with each photograph, develop the film in the darkroom, and edit the film for production. For large photo-essay assignments, they research the subject matter and supervise the layout of the pages. Since most newspapers are now laid out on computers, today's photojournalists download or scan their pictures into a computer and save images on disks.

More often than not, photojournalists use digital cameras to eliminate the need for developing and scanning film. Since the debut of the first digital camera designed for newspapers in the early 1990s, digital photography has revolutionized photojournalism. Unlike traditional film cameras, digital cameras use electronic memory rather than a negative to record an image. The image can then be downloaded instantly into a computer and sent worldwide via e-mail or by posting it on the Internet. By eliminating developing and transportation time, digital cameras allow a sports photographer to shoot a picture of the game-winning basket and immediately transmit it to a newspaper hundreds of miles away before a late-night deadline.

Some photojournalists work on the staffs of weekly or daily newspapers, while others take photographs for magazines or specialty journals. Most magazines employ only a few or no photographic staff, but depend on freelance photojournalists to provide their pictures. Magazine photojournalists sometimes specialize in a specific field, such as sports or food photography.

Some photographers and photojournalists write for trade and technical journals, teach photography in schools and colleges, act as representatives of photographic equipment manufacturers, sell photographic equipment and supplies, produce documentary films, or do freelance work.

REQUIREMENTS

High School

While in high school, take as many art classes and photography classes that are available. Chemistry is useful for understanding developing and printing processes. You can learn about photo manipulation software and digital photography in computer classes, and business classes will help if you are considering a freelance career.

If you decide to specialize in photojournalism, you will need a well-rounded education. Take classes in English, foreign language, history, and the sciences to prepare yourself for the job.

Postsecondary Training

Formal educational requirements depend upon the nature of the photographer's specialty. For instance, photographic work in scientific and engineering research generally requires an engineering background with a degree from a recognized college or institute.

A college education is not required to become a photographer or photojournalist, although college training probably offers the most promising assurance of success in fields such as industrial, news, or scientific photography. There are degree programs at the associate's, bachelor's, and master's levels. Many, however, become photographers with no formal education beyond high school.

Many journalism programs require their students to complete internships with newspapers or other local employers. This is essential to building your experience and getting a good job in this competitive field. Many photojournalists are offered their first jobs directly from their internship experience.

Other Requirements

You should possess manual dexterity, good eyesight and color vision, and artistic ability to succeed in this line of work. You need an eye for form and line, an appreciation of light and shadow, and the ability to use imaginative and creative approaches to photographs or film, especially in commercial work. In addition, you should be patient and accurate and enjoy working with detail.

Self-employed (or freelance) photographers need good business skills. They must be able to manage their own studios, including hiring and managing assistants and other employees, keeping records, and maintaining photographic and business files. Marketing and sales skills are also important to a successful freelance photography business.

Because of the timely nature of many assignments, photojournalists must be able to work under the pressures of a deadline. They may be assigned to shoot pictures of people in trying situations, such as house fires, car wrecks, or military combat. In these cases, the photojournalist must be extremely sensitive to the people at the center of the story, ask permission to take photos, and when possible, ask for details about what happened. To do this, photojournalists must be extremely tactful and polite and work well under stress.

EXPLORING

Photography is a field that anyone with a camera can explore. To learn more about this career, you can join high school camera clubs, yearbook or newspaper staffs, photography contests, and community hobby groups. You can also seek a part-time or summer job in a camera shop or work as a developer in a laboratory or processing center.

EMPLOYERS

About 129,000 photographers and photojournalists work in the United States, more than half of whom are self-employed. Most jobs for photographers are provided by photographic or commercial art studios; other employers include newspapers and magazines, radio and TV broadcasting, government agencies, and manufacturing firms. Colleges, universities, and other educational institutions employ photographers to prepare promotional and educational materials.

A large percentage of photojournalists work as freelance contractors. Photo agencies and news organizations such as the Associated Press purchase photos from freelance photojournalists to use in print and online publications. Some photojournalists work on staff for newspapers, magazines, or other print publications. Television networks also hire photojournalists to help illustrate breaking stories.

STARTING OUT

Some photographers enter the field as apprentices, trainees, or assistants. Trainees may work in a darkroom, camera shop, or developing laboratory. They may move lights and arrange backgrounds for a commercial or portrait photographer. Assistants spend many months learning this kind of work before they move into a job behind a camera.

Many large cities offer schools of photography, which may be a good way to start in the field. Beginning photojournalists may work for one of the many newspapers and magazines published in their area. Other photographers choose to go into business for themselves as soon as they have finished their formal education. Setting up a studio may not require a large capital outlay, but beginners may find that success does not come easily.

ADVANCEMENT

Because photography is such a diversified field, there is no usual way in which to get ahead. Those who begin by working for someone else may advance to owning their own businesses. Commercial photographers may gain prestige as more of their pictures are placed in well-known trade journals or popular magazines. Photojournalists can advance by shooting for more prestigious papers (and earning more money for it) or by going into business on their own. They can advance to become the head photo editor, in charge of a staff of photojournalists, or they can even become managing editors or editors in chief of a publication. Other newspaper photojournalists move into magazine photography, usually on a freelance basis. Where newspaper photojournalists are generalists, magazine photography is usually more specific in nature. A few photographers may become celebrities in their own right by making contributions to the art world or the sciences.

EARNINGS

The U.S. Department of Labor reports that salaried photographers employed by newspaper, book, and directory publishers earned mean annual salaries of $37,230 in 2005. Salaries for all photographers ranged from less than $15,240 to more than $53,900.

Self-employed photographers often earn more than salaried photographers, but their earnings depend on general business conditions. In addition, self-employed photographers do not receive the benefits that a company provides its employees.

Photographers in salaried jobs usually receive benefits such as paid holidays, vacations, and sick leave and medical insurance.

WORK ENVIRONMENT

Work conditions vary based on the job and employer. Many photographers work a 35- to 40-hour workweek, but freelancers and news photographers often put in long, irregular hours. Commercial and portrait photographers work in comfortable surroundings. Photojournalists seldom are assured physical comfort in their work and may in fact face danger when covering stories on natural disasters or military conflicts. Some photographers work in research laboratory

A high school photojournalism student practices taking photographs with a tripod. *(The Image Works)*

settings; others work on aircraft; and still others work underwater. For some photographers, conditions change from day to day. One day, they may be photographing a hot and dusty rodeo; the next they may be taking pictures of a dog sled race in Alaska.

In general, photographers work under pressure to meet deadlines and satisfy customers. Freelance photographers have the added pressure of uncertain incomes and have to continually seek out new clients.

For freelance photographers, the cost of equipment can be quite expensive, with no assurance that the money spent will be repaid through income from future assignments. Freelancers in travel-related photography, such as travel and tourism photographers and photojournalists, have the added cost of transportation and accommodations. For all photographers, flexibility is a major asset.

OUTLOOK

Employment of photographers and photojournalists will increase about as fast as the average for all occupations through 2014, according to the *Occupational Outlook Handbook*. The demand for new images should remain strong in education, communication, entertainment, marketing, and research. As the Internet grows and more newspapers and magazines turn to electronic publishing, demand will increase for photographers to produce digital images.

Photography is a highly competitive field. There are far more photographers and photojournalists than positions available. Only those who are extremely talented and highly skilled can support themselves as self-employed workers in these professions. Many photographers and photojournalists take pictures as a sideline while working another job.

FOR MORE INFORMATION

The ASMP promotes the rights of photographers and photojournalists, educates its members in business practices, and promotes high standards of ethics.
American Society of Media Photographers (ASMP)
150 North Second Street
Philadelphia, PA 19106-1912
Tel: 215-451-2767
http://www.asmp.org

The NPPA maintains a job bank, provides educational information, and makes insurance available to its members. It also publishes News Photographer *magazine.*
National Press Photographers Association (NPPA)
3200 Croasdaile Drive, Suite 306
Durham, NC 27705-2588
Tel: 919-383-7246
Email: info@nppa.org
http://www.nppa.org

This organization provides training, publishes its own magazine, and offers various services for its members.
Professional Photographers of America
229 Peachtree Street, NE, Suite 2200
Atlanta, GA 30303-1608
Tel: 800-786-6277
Email: csc@ppa.com
http://www.ppa.com

For information on student membership, contact
Student Photographic Society
229 Peachtree Street, NE, Suite 2200
Atlanta, GA 30303-1608
Tel: 866-886-5325
Email: info@studentphoto.com
http://www.studentphoto.com

Prepress Workers

OVERVIEW

Prepress workers handle the first stage in the printing process. This initial phase of production involves multiple steps, including creating pages from text and graphics and making printing plates. With the introduction of desktop publishing and other computer technology, the prepress process has changed dramatically over the past decade. Computerized processes have replaced many of the traditional processes, eliminating a number of prepress jobs but opening up new opportunities as well.

According to the U.S. Department of Labor, 141,000 people are employed in prepress jobs. Approximately 42,000 of these jobs are with commercial printing companies. Other jobs are with prepress service bureaus (companies that deal exclusively with prepress work) and newspapers.

HISTORY

The history of modern printing began with the invention of movable type in the 15th century. For several centuries before that, books had been printed from carved wooden blocks or laboriously copied by hand. These painstaking methods of production were so expensive that books were chained to prevent theft.

In the 1440s, Johannes Gutenberg invented a form of metal type that could be used over and over. The first known book to be printed with this movable type was a Bible in 1455—the now-famous Gutenberg Bible. Gutenberg's revolutionary new type greatly reduced the time and cost involved in printing, and books soon became plentiful.

Ottmar Mergenthaler, a German immigrant to the United States, invented the Linotype machine in 1886. Linotype allowed the typesetter to set type from a keyboard that used a mechanical device to set letters in place. Before this, printers were setting type by hand, one letter at a time, picking up each letter individually from their typecases as they had been doing for more than 400 years. At about the same time, Tolbert Lanston invented the Monotype machine, which also had a keyboard but set the type as individual letters. These inventions allowed compositors to set type much faster and more efficiently.

With these machines, newspapers advanced from the small two-page weeklies of the 1700s to the huge editions of today's metropolitan dailies. The volume of other periodicals, advertisements, books, and other printed matter also proliferated.

In the 1950s, a new system called photocomposition was introduced into commercial typesetting operations. In this system, typesetting machines used photographic images of letters, which were projected onto a photosensitive surface to compose pages. Instructions to the typesetting machine about which letters to project and where to project them were fed in through a punched-paper or magnetic tape, which was, in turn, created by an operator at a keyboard.

Most recently, typesetting has come into the home and office in the form of desktop publishing. This process has revolutionized the industry by enabling companies and individuals to do their own type composition and graphic design work.

THE JOB

Prepress work involves a variety of tasks, most of which are now computer-based. The prepress process is typically broken down into the following areas of responsibility: compositor and typesetter, paste-up worker, desktop publishing specialist, pre-flight technician, output technician, scanner operator, camera operator, lithographic artist, film stripper, and platemaker.

Compositors and *typesetters* are responsible for setting up and arranging type by hand or by computer into galleys for printing. This is done using "cold type" technology (as opposed to the old "hot type" method, which involved using molten lead to create letters and lines of text). A common method is phototypesetting, in which type is entered into a computer and output on photographic film or paper. Typesetting in its traditional sense requires a *paste-up worker* to then position illustrations and layout columns of type. This manual process is quickly being phased out by desktop publishing.

Most often today, desktop publishing is the first step in the production process. The *desktop publisher* designs and lays out text and graphics on a personal computer according to the specifications of the job. This involves sizing text, setting column widths, and arranging copy with photos and other images. All elements of the piece are displayed on the computer screen and manipulated using a keyboard and mouse. In commercial printing plants, jobs tend to come from customers on computer disk, eliminating the need for initial desktop publishing work on the part of the printing company. The entire electronic file is reviewed by the *pre-flight technician* to ensure that all of its elements are properly formatted and set up. At small print shops—which account for the majority of the printing industry—a *job printer* is often the person in charge of typesetting, page layout, proofing copy, and fixing problems with files.

Once a file is ready, the *output technician* transmits it through an imagesetter onto paper, film, or directly to a plate. The latter method is called digital imaging, and it bypasses the film stage altogether. Direct-to-plate technology has been adopted by a growing number of printing companies nationwide.

If a file is output onto paper or provided camera-ready, the *camera operator* photographs the material and develops film negatives, either by hand or by machine. Because the bulk of commercial printing today is done using lithography, most camera operators can also be called *lithographic photographers.*

Often it is necessary to make corrections, change or reshape images, or lighten or darken the film negatives. This is the job of the *lithographic artist,* who, depending on the area of specialty, might have the title *dot etcher, retoucher,* or *letterer.* This film retouching work is highly specialized and is all done by hand using chemicals, dyes, and special tools.

The *film stripper* is the person who cuts film negatives to the proper size and arranges them onto large sheets called flats. The pieces are taped into place so that they are in proper position for the plate to be made.

The *platemaker,* also called a *lithographer* because of the process used in most commercial plants, creates the printing plates. This is done using a photographic process. The film is laid on top of a thin metal plate treated with a light-sensitive chemical. It is exposed to ultraviolet light, which "burns" the positive image into the plate. Those areas are then chemically treated so that when ink is applied to the plate, it adheres to the images to be printed and is repelled by the nonprinting areas.

Lithography work traditionally involved sketching designs on stone, clay, or glass. Some of these older methods are still used for specialized purposes, but the predominant method today is the one previously described, which is used in offset printing. In offset printing, a series of cylinders are used to transfer ink from the chemically treated plate onto a rubber cylinder (called a blanket), then onto the paper. The printing plate never touches the paper but is "offset" by the rubber blanket.

If photos and art are not provided electronically, the *scanner operator* scans them using a high-resolution drum or flatbed scanner. In the scanning process, the continuous color tone of the original image is interpreted electronically and converted into a combination of the four primary colors used in printing: cyan (blue), magenta, yellow, and black—commonly called CMYK. A screening process separates the image into the four colors, each of which is represented by a series of dots called a halftone. These halftones are recorded to film from which printing plates are made. During the printing process, ink applied to each of the plates combines on paper to recreate the color of the original image.

REQUIREMENTS

Educational requirements for prepress workers vary according to the area of responsibility, but all require at least a high school diploma, and most call for a strong command of computers.

Whereas prepress areas used to be typesetting and hand-composition operations run by people skilled in particular crafts, they are now predominantly computer-based. Workers are no longer quite as specialized and generally are competent in a variety of tasks. Thus, one of the most important criteria for prepress workers today is a solid base of computer knowledge, ideally in programs and processes related to graphic design and prepress work.

High School
Young people interested in the field are advised to take courses in computer science, mathematics, and electronics.

Postsecondary Training
The more traditional jobs, such as camera operator, film stripper, lithographic artist, and platemaker, require longer, more specialized preparation. This might involve an apprenticeship or a two-year associate's degree. But these jobs now are on the decline as they are replaced by computerized processes.

Postsecondary education is strongly encouraged for most prepress positions and a requirement for some jobs, including any managerial role. Graphic arts programs are offered by community and junior colleges as well as four-year colleges and universities. Postsecondary programs in printing technology are also available.

Any programs or courses that give you exposure to the printing field will be an asset. Courses in printing are often available at vocational-technical institutes and through printing trade associations.

Certification or Licensing
The National Council for Skill Standards in Graphic Communications has established a list of competencies for workers in the printing industry. To demonstrate their knowledge, operators can take examinations in flexographic press operation, offset sheetfed and web press operation, finishing and stitching, and imaging. Applicants receive the national council certified operator designation for each examination that they successfully complete.

Other Requirements
Prepress work requires strong communications skills, attention to detail, and the ability to perform well in a high-pressure, deadline-driven environment. Physically, you should have good manual dexterity, good eyesight, and overall visual perception. Artistic skill is an advantage in nearly any prepress job.

EXPLORING

A summer job or internship doing basic word processing or desktop publishing is one way to get a feel for what prepress work involves. Such an opportunity could even be found through a temporary agency. Of course, you will need a knowledge of computers and certain software.

You also can volunteer to do desktop publishing or design work for your school newspaper or yearbook. This would have the added benefit of exposing you to the actual printing process.

EMPLOYERS

There are approximately 141,000 prepress workers employed in the United States. Most prepress work is in firms that do commercial or business printing and in newspaper plants. Other jobs are at companies that specialize in certain aspects of the prepress process, for example, platemaking or outputting of film.

Because printing is so widespread, prepress jobs are available in almost any part of the country. However, according to the *Occupational Outlook Handbook,* prepress work is concentrated in large printing centers like New York, Chicago, Los Angeles-Long Beach, Philadelphia, Minneapolis-St. Paul, Boston, and Washington, D.C.

STARTING OUT

Information on apprenticeships and training opportunities is available through state employment services and local chapters of printing industry associations.

If you wish to start working first and learn your skills on the job you should contact potential employers directly, especially if you want to work in a small nonunion print shop. Openings for trainee positions may be listed in newspaper want ads or with the state employment service. Trade school graduates may find jobs through their school's career services office. And industry association offices often run job listing services.

ADVANCEMENT

Some prepress work, such as typesetting, can be learned fairly quickly; other jobs, like film stripping or platemaking, take years to master. Workers often begin as assistants and move into on-the-job training programs. Entry-level workers are trained by more experienced workers and advance according to how quickly they learn and prove themselves.

In larger companies, prepress workers can move up the ranks to take on supervisory roles. Prepress and production work is also a good starting point for people who aim to become a customer service or sales representative for a printing company.

EARNINGS

Pay rates vary for prepress workers, depending on their level of experience and responsibility, type of company, where they live, and whether or not they are union members. Prepress technicians and workers had median annual earnings of $32,840 in 2005. Salaries ranged from less than $19,430 to $52,800 or more. Mean earnings in commercial printing, the industry employing the largest number of prepress technicians and workers, were $34,820. Those employed in newspaper, book, and directory publishing had mean annual earnings of $33,560.

WORK ENVIRONMENT

Generally, prepress workers work in clean, quiet settings away from the noise and activity of the pressroom. Prepress areas are usually air-conditioned and roomy. Desktop publishers and others who work in front of computer terminals can risk straining their eyes, as well as their backs and necks. Film stripping and other detail-oriented work also can be tiring to the eyes. The chemicals used in platemaking can irritate the skin.

Newsroom Diversity, 2005

- Minorities comprised 13.87 percent of newsroom staff in 2005—an increase of 1.80 percent from 2002, but far less than the minority representation (33 percent) in the general population.
- Minorities make up 11.2 percent of all managers in newsrooms.
- Newspapers having a circulation of 100,000 to 250,000 employ the highest percentage (25 percent) of minority journalists.
- Women make up 37.7 percent of newsroom staff.

Source: American Society of Newspaper Editors

An eight-hour day is typical for most prepress jobs, but frequently workers put in more than eight hours. Prepress jobs at newspapers and financial printers often call for weekend and evening hours.

OUTLOOK

Overall employment in the prepress portion of the printing industry is expected to decline through 2014, according to the U.S. Department of Labor. While it is anticipated that the demand for printed materials will increase, prepress work will not, mainly because of new innovations.

Almost all prepress operations are computerized, and many of the traditional jobs that involved highly skilled handwork—film strippers, paste-up workers, photoengravers, camera operators, and platemakers—are being phased out. The computer-oriented aspects of prepress work have replaced most of these tasks. Employment of desktop publishing specialists, however, is expected to grow faster than the average. Demand for pre-flight technicians will also be strong. And specialized computer skills will increasingly be needed to handle direct to plate and other new technology.

Given the increasing demand for rush print jobs, printing trade service companies should offer good opportunities for prepress workers. Larger companies and companies not equipped for specialized prepress work will continue to turn to these specialty shops to keep up with their workload.

FOR MORE INFORMATION

This organization offers information, services, and training related to printing, electronic prepress, electronic publishing, and other areas of the graphic arts industry.

Graphic Arts Information Network
Printing Industries of America/Graphic Arts Technical Foundation

200 Deer Run Road
Sewickley, PA 15143-2600
Tel: 800-910-4283
Email: gain@piagatf.org
http://www.gain.net

This organization represents U.S. and Canadian workers in all craft and skill areas of the printing and publishing industries. In addition to developing cooperative relationships with employers, it also offers education and training through local union schools.

**Graphic Communications Conference of the International
Brotherhood of Teamsters**
1900 L Street, NW
Washington, DC 20036-5002
Tel: 202-462-1400
http://www.gciu.org

This trade association of graphic communications and graphic arts supplier companies offers economic and management information, publications, and industry reports and studies.

IPA-The Association of Graphic Solutions Providers
7200 France Avenue South, Suite 223
Edina, MN 55435-4309
Tel: 800-255-8141
http://www.ipa.org

This graphic arts trade association is a good source of general information.

National Association for Printing Leadership
75 West Century Road
Paramus, NJ 07652-1408
Tel: 800-642-6275
http://www.napl.org

For information on certification, contact
The Printing Industries of Wisconsin
National Council for Skill Standards in Graphic Communications
Harry V. Quadracci Printing & Graphic Center
800 Main Street
Pewaukee, WI 53072-4601
http://www.ncssgc.org

For information on careers and educational institutions, visit
Graphic Comm Central
http://teched.vt.edu/gcc

Printing Press Operators and Assistants

OVERVIEW

Printing press operators and printing press operator assistants prepare, operate, and maintain printing presses. Their principal duties include installing and adjusting printing plates, loading and feeding paper, mixing inks and controlling ink flow, and ensuring the quality of the final printed piece.

There are approximately 191,000 printing press operators in the United States. They are mostly employed by newspaper plants and commercial and business printers.

HISTORY

The forerunners of today's modern printing presses were developed in Germany in the 15th century. They made use of the new concept of movable type, an invention generally credited to Johannes Gutenberg. Before Gutenberg's time, most books were copied by hand or printed from carved wooden blocks. Movable type used separate pieces of metal that could be easily set in place, locked into a form for printing, and then used again for another job.

The first presses consisted of two flat surfaces. Once set in place, the type was inked with a roller, and a sheet of paper was pressed against the type with a lever. Two people working together could print about 300 pages a day.

In the early 19th century, Friedrich Konig, another German, developed the first cylinder press. With a cylinder press, the paper is mounted on a large cylinder that is rolled over a flat printing surface.

The first rotary press was developed in the United States in 1865 by William Bullock. On this kind of press, the inked surface is on a revolving cylinder called a plate cylinder. The plate cylinder acts like a roller and prints onto a continuous sheet of paper (called a web) coming off a giant roll.

The speed and economy of the web press was improved by the discovery of offset printing in the early 20th century. In this process, the raised metal type used in earlier processes was substituted with a flexible plate that could be easily attached to the plate cylinder. The ink is transferred from the plate onto a rubber cylinder (called a blanket), then onto the paper. The printing plate never touches the paper but is "offset" by the rubber blanket.

Offset printing uses the process of lithography, in which the plate is chemically treated so that ink sticks only to the parts that are to be printed and is repelled by the nonprint areas.

Offset lithography is the most common form of printing today and is used on both webfed and sheetfed presses. Webfed presses are used for newspapers and other large-volume, lower-cost runs. The fastest web presses today can print about 150,000 complete newspapers in an hour. Sheetfed presses, which print on single sheets of paper rather than a continuous roll, are used for smaller, higher-quality jobs.

Other forms of printing are gravure (in which depressions on an etched plate are inked and pressed to paper), flexography (a form of rotary printing using flexible rubber plates with raised image areas and fast-drying inks), and letterpress (the most traditional method, in which a plate with raised, inked images is pressed against paper).

THE JOB

The duties of press operators and their assistants vary according to the size of the printing plant in which they work. Generally, they are involved in all aspects of making the presses ready for a job and monitoring and operating the presses during the print run. Because most presses now are computerized, the work of press operators involves both electronic and manual processes.

In small shops, press operators usually handle all of the tasks associated with running a press, including cleaning and oiling the parts and making minor repairs. In larger shops, press operators are aided by assistants who handle most maintenance and cleanup tasks.

A pressroom manager stands at a control panel making adjustments to an offset press. *(The Image Works)*

Once the press has been inspected and the printing plate arrives from the platemaker, the "makeready" process begins. In this stage, the operators mount the plates into place on the printing surface or cylinder. They mix and match the ink, fill the ink fountains, and adjust the ink flow and dampening systems. They also load the paper, adjust the press to the paper size, feed the paper through the cylinders and, on a web press, adjust the tension controls. When this is done, a proof sheet is run off for the customer's review.

When the proof has been approved and final adjustments have been made, the press run begins. During the run, press operators constantly check the quality of the printed sheets and make any necessary adjustments. They look to see that the print is clear and properly positioned and that ink is not offsetting (blotting) onto other sheets. If the job involves color, they make sure that the colors line up properly with the images they are assigned to (registration). Operators also monitor the chemical properties of the ink and correct temperatures in the drying chamber, if the press has one.

On a web press, the feeding and tension mechanisms must be continually monitored. If the paper tears or jams, it must be rethreaded. As a roll of paper runs out, a new one must be spliced onto the old one. Some web presses today can print up to 50,000 feet an hour. At this rate, the press might run through a giant roll of paper every half hour. In large web printing plants, it takes an entire crew of specialized operators to oversee the process.

Most printing plants now have computerized printing presses equipped with sophisticated instrumentation. Press operators work at a control panel that monitors the printing processes and can adjust each variable automatically.

REQUIREMENTS

High School

The minimum educational requirement for printing press operators and assistants is a high school diploma. Students interested in this field should take courses that offer an introduction to printing and color theory, as well as chemistry, computer science, electronics, mathematics, and physics—any course that develops mechanical and mathematical aptitude.

Postsecondary Training

Traditionally, press operators learned their craft through apprenticeship programs ranging from four to five years. Apprenticeships are still available, but they are being phased out by postsecondary programs in printing equipment operation offered by technical and trade schools and community and junior colleges. Information on apprenticeships is often available through state employment services and local chapters of printing industry associations. Additionally, many press operators and assistants still receive informal on-the-job training after they are hired by a printer.

Computer training is also essential to be successful in the printing industry today. With today's rapid advances in technology, "students need all the computer knowledge they can get," advises John Smotherman, press operator and shift supervisor at Busch and Schmidt Company in Broadview, Illinois.

Certification or Licensing

The National Council for Skill Standards in Graphic Communications has established a list of competencies—what an operator should know and be able to do—for the expert level of performance. Skill standards are available for electronic imaging, sheetfed and web offset press, flexographic press, and finishing and stitching. Operators who take one or more examination in these subjects areas can receive the designation national council certified operator.

Other Requirements

Strong communication skills, both verbal and written, are a must for press operators and assistants. They also must be able to work well as a team, both with each other and with others in the printing company. Any miscommunication during the printing process can be costly if it means rerunning a job or any part of it. Working well under pressure is another requirement because most print jobs run on tight deadlines.

EXPLORING

High school is a good time to begin exploring the occupation of printing press operator. Some schools offer print shop classes, which provide the most direct exposure to this work. Working on the high school newspaper or yearbook is another way to gain a familiarity with the printing process. A delivery job with a print shop or a visit to a local printing plant will offer you the chance to see presses in action and get a feel for the environment in which press operators work. You also might consider a part-time, temporary, or summer job as a cleanup worker or press feeder in a printing plant.

EMPLOYERS

There are approximately 191,000 press operators employed in the United States. The bulk of these are with newspapers and commercial and business printers. Companies range from small print shops, where one or two press operators handle everything, to large corporations that employ teams of press operators to work around the clock.

Other press operator jobs are with in-plant operations, that is, in companies and organizations that do their own printing in-house.

Because printing is so geographically diverse, press operator jobs are available in almost any city or town in the country. However, according to the *Occupational Outlook Handbook*, press work is concentrated in large printing centers like New York, Chicago, Los Angeles-Long Beach, Philadelphia, Minneapolis-St. Paul, Boston, and Washington, D.C.

STARTING OUT

Openings for trainee positions may be listed in newspaper want ads or with the state employment service. Trade school graduates may find jobs through their school's career services office. And industry association offices often run job listing services.

John Smotherman notes that many young people entering the field start out in a part-time position while still in school. "I think students should pursue all the classroom education they can, but many intricacies of the printing process, like how certain inks and papers work together, need to be learned through experience," he says.

ADVANCEMENT

Most printing press operators, even those with some training, begin their careers doing entry-level work, such as loading, unloading, and cleaning the presses. In large print shops, the line of promotion is usually as follows: press helper, press assistant, press operator, press operator-in-charge, pressroom supervisor, superintendent.

Press operators can advance in salary and responsibility level by learning to work more complex printing equipment, for example by moving from a one-color press to a four-color press. Printing press operators should be prepared to continue their training and education throughout their careers. As printing companies upgrade their equipment and buy new, more computerized presses, retraining will be essential.

Press operators who are interested in other aspects of the printing business also may find advancement opportunities elsewhere in their company. Those with business savvy may be successful in establishing their own print shops.

EARNINGS

Pay rates vary for press operators, depending on their level of experience and responsibility, type of company, where they live, and whether or not they are union members. Median annual earnings of press operators were $30,730 in 2005, according to the U.S. Department of Labor (USDL). Salaries ranged from less than $18,450 to $49,870 or more. The USDL reports the following annual mean earnings for printing press operators by industry: printing and related support activities, $33,550; newspaper, book, and directory publishing, $36,280; converted paper product manufacturing, $34,220; and advertising and related services, $27,560.

WORK ENVIRONMENT

Pressrooms are well ventilated, well lit, and humidity controlled. They are also noisy. Often press operators must wear ear protectors. Presswork can be physically strenuous and requires a lot of standing. Press operators also have considerable contact with ink and cleaning fluids that can cause skin and eye irritation.

Working around large machines can be hazardous, so press operators must constantly observe good safety habits.

An eight-hour day is typical for most press operators, but some work longer hours. Smaller plants generally have only a day shift, but many larger plants and newspaper printers run around the clock. At these plants, like in hospitals and factories, press operator shifts are broken into day, afternoon/evening, and "graveyard" hours.

OUTLOOK

The U.S. Department of Labor predicts that employment of press operators will grow more slowly than the average for all occupations through 2014. An increased demand for printed materials—advertising, direct mail pieces, computer software packaging, books, and magazines—will be offset by the use of larger, more efficient machines. Additionally, new business practices such as printing-on-demand (where materials are printed in smaller amounts as they are requested by customers instead of being printed in large runs that may not be used) and electronic publishing (which is the publication of materials on the Internet or through other electronic methods of dissemination) will also limit opportunities for workers in this field.

Newcomers to the field are likely to encounter stiff competition from experienced workers or workers who have completed retraining programs to update their skills. Opportunities are expected to be greatest for students who have completed formal apprenticeships or postsecondary training programs.

FOR MORE INFORMATION

For information on flexographic printing, contact
Flexographic Technical Association
900 Marconi Avenue
Ronkonkoma, NY 11779-7212
Tel: 631-737-6020
http://www.flexography.org

This organization offers information, services, and training related to printing, electronic prepress, electronic publishing, and other areas of the graphic arts industry.
Graphic Arts Information Network
Printing Industries of America/Graphic Arts Technical Foundation
200 Deer Run Road
Sewickley, PA 15143-2600
Tel: 800-910-4283
Email: gain@piagatf.org
http://www.gain.net

This organization represents U.S. and Canadian workers in all craft and skill areas of the printing and publishing industries. In addition to developing cooperative relationships with employers, it also offers education and training through local union schools.

Graphic Communications Conference of the International Brotherhood of Teamsters
1900 L Street, NW
Washington, DC 20036-5002
Tel: 202-462-1400
http://www.gciu.org

This trade association of graphic communications and graphic arts supplier companies offers economic and management information, publications, and industry reports and studies.

IPA-The Association of Graphic Solutions Providers
7200 France Avenue South, Suite 223
Edina, MN 55435-4309
Tel: 800-255-8141
http://www.ipa.org

This graphic arts trade association is a good source of general information.

National Association for Printing Leadership
75 West Century Road
Paramus, NJ 07652-1408
Tel: 800-642-6275
http://www.napl.org

For more information on the national council certified operator designation, contact

The Printing Industries of Wisconsin
National Council for Skill Standards in Graphic Communications
Harry V. Quadracci Printing & Graphic Center
800 Main Street
Pewaukee WI 53072-4601
Tel: 262-695-6251
http://www.ncssgc.org

For information on careers and educational institutions, visit

Graphic Comm Central
http://teched.vt.edu/gcc

Public Opinion Researchers

OVERVIEW

Public opinion researchers help measure public sentiment about various products, services, or social issues by gathering information from a sample of the population through questionnaires and interviews. They collect, analyze, and interpret data and opinions to explore issues and forecast trends. Their poll results help business people, politicians, and other decision makers determine what's on the public's mind. It is estimated that there are fewer than 100,000 full-time employees currently in the field, primarily working for the government or private industry in large cities.

HISTORY

Public opinion research began in a rudimentary way in the 1830s and 1840s when local newspapers asked their readers to fill out unofficial ballots indicating for whom they had voted in a particular election. Since that time, research on political issues has been conducted with increasing frequency—especially during presidential election years. However, public opinion research is most widely used by businesses to determine what products or services consumers like or dislike.

As questionnaires and interviewing techniques have become more refined, the field of public opinion research has become more accurate at reflecting the individual attitudes and opinions of the sample groups. Companies like The Gallup Organization and Harris Interactive conduct surveys for a wide range of political and economic purposes. Although some people continue to question the accuracy and importance of polls, they have become an integral part of our social fabric.

THE JOB

Public opinion researchers conduct interviews and gather data that accurately reflect public opinions. They do this so decision makers in the business and political worlds have a better idea of what people want on a wide range of issues. Public opinion is sometimes gauged by interviewing a small percentage of the population containing a variety of people who closely parallel the larger population in terms of age, race, income, and other factors. At other times, researchers interview people who represent a certain demographic group. Public opinion researchers may help a company implement a new marketing strategy or help a political candidate decide which campaign issues the public considers important.

Researchers use a variety of methods to collect and analyze public opinion. The particular method depends on the target audience and the type of information desired. For example, if a newspaper is interested in gauging the opinions of teen readers, the research company will most likely station interviewers in selected areas—such as shopping malls, fast-food restaurants, or parks—where young people are known to congregate. On the other hand, an advertising firm may be interested in the opinions of a particular demographic group, such as working mothers or teenagers. In this case, the research firm would plan a procedure (such as a telephone survey) providing access to that group. Other field collection methods include interviews in the home and at work as well as questionnaires that are filled out by respondents and then returned through the mail.

Planning is an important ingredient in developing an effective survey method. After they receive an assignment, researchers decide what portion of the population they will survey and develop questions that will result in an accurate gauging of opinion. Researchers investigate whether previous surveys have been done on a particular topic, and if so, what the results were.

It is important that exactly the same procedures be used throughout the entire data collection process so that the survey is not influenced by the individual styles of the interviewers. For this reason, the process is closely monitored by supervisory personnel. *Research assistants* help train survey interviewers, prepare survey questionnaires and related materials, and tabulate and code survey results.

Other specialists within the field include *market research analysts,* who collect, analyze, and interpret survey results to determine what they mean. They prepare reports and make recommendations on subjects ranging from preferences of prospective customers to future sales trends. They use mathematical and statistical models to analyze research. Research analysts are careful to screen out unimportant or invalid information that could skew their survey results. (For more information on this career, see the article "Marketing Research Analysts.") *Survey workers* conduct public opinion interviews to determine people's buying habits or opinions on public issues. Survey workers contact people in their homes, at work, at random in public places, or via the telephone, questioning the person in a specified manner, usually following a questionnaire format.

At times public opinion researchers are mistaken for telemarketers. According to the Council for Marketing and Opinion Research, public opinion researchers are conducting serious research, collecting opinions whereas telemarketers ultimately are in the business of sales.

REQUIREMENTS

High School
Because the ability to communicate in both spoken and written form is crucial for this job, you should take courses in English, speech arts, and social studies while in high school. In addition, take mathematics (especially statistics) and any courses in journalism or psychology that are available. Knowledge of a foreign language is also helpful.

Postsecondary Training
A college degree in economics or business administration provides a good background for public opinion researchers. A degree in sociology or psychology will be helpful for those interested in studying consumer demand or opinion research, while work in statistics or engineering might be more useful for those interested in certain types of industrial or analytical research.

Because of the increasingly sophisticated techniques used in public opinion research, most employers expect researchers to be familiar with computer applications, and many require a master's degree in business administration, sociology, educational psychology, or political science. While a doctorate is not necessary for most researchers, it is highly desirable for those who plan to become involved with complex research studies or work in an academic environment.

Other Requirements
Public opinion researchers who conduct interviews must be outgoing and enjoy interacting with a wide variety of people. Because much

of the work involves getting people to reveal their personal opinions and beliefs, you must be a good listener and as nonjudgmental as possible. You must be patient and be able to handle rejection because some people may be uncooperative during the interviewing process.

If you choose to work in data analysis, you should be able to pay close attention to detail and spend long hours analyzing complex data. You may experience some pressure when forced to collect data or solve a problem within a specified period of time. If you intend to plan questionnaires, you will need good analytical skills and a strong command of the English language.

EXPLORING

High school students can often work as survey workers for a telemarketing firm or other consumer research company. Work opportunities may also be available where you can learn about the coding and tabulation of survey data. Actual participation in a consumer survey may also offer insight into the type of work involved in the field. You should also try to talk with professionals already working in the field to learn more about the profession.

EMPLOYERS

Fewer than 100,000 full-time public opinion researchers are employed in the field. Public opinion workers are primarily employed by private companies, such as public and private research firms and advertising agencies. They also work for the government and for various colleges and universities, often in research and teaching capacities. As is usually the case, those with the most experience and education should find the greatest number of job opportunities. Gaining experience in a specific area can give prospective researchers an edge.

STARTING OUT

Many people enter the field in a support position such as a survey worker, and with experience become interviewers or work as data analysts. Those with applicable education, training, and experience may begin as interviewers or data analysts. College career services counselors can often help qualified students find an appropriate position in public opinion research. Contacts can also be made through summer employment or by locating public and private research companies in the phone book.

ADVANCEMENT

Advancement opportunities are numerous in the public opinion research field. Often a research assistant will be promoted to a position as an interviewer or data analyst and, after sufficient experience in these or other aspects of research project development, become involved in a supervisory or planning capacity.

With a master's degree or doctorate, a person can become a manager of a large private research organization or marketing research director for an industrial or business firm. Those with extended work experience in public opinion research and with sufficient credentials may choose to start their own companies. Opportunities also exist in university teaching or research and development.

EARNINGS

Starting salaries vary according to the skill and experience of the applicant, the nature of the position, and the size of the company. The U.S. Department of Labor (USDL) does not offer salary information for public opinion researchers. It does report that market research analysts (a type of public opinion researcher) earned a median salary of $57,300 in 2005. Earnings ranged from less than $31,530 to $108,990 or more. The department also reports that survey workers earned salaries in 2005 that ranged from less than $16,080 to more than $70,450. The median annual salary for survey workers was $31,140 in 2005.

Most full-time public opinion researchers receive the usual medical, pension, vacation, and other benefits that other professional workers do. Managers may also receive bonuses based on their company's performance.

WORK ENVIRONMENT

Public opinion researchers usually work a standard 40-hour week, although they may have to work overtime occasionally if a project has a tight deadline. Those in supervisory positions may work especially long hours overseeing the collection and interpretation of information.

When conducting telephone interviews or organizing or analyzing data, researchers work in comfortable offices, with typewriters, calculators, computers, and data processing equipment close at hand. When collecting information via personal interviews or questionnaires, it is not unusual to spend time outside in shopping malls, on the street, or in private homes. Some evening and weekend work may be involved because people are most readily available to be interviewed at those times. Some research positions may include assignments that involve travel, but these are generally short assignments.

OUTLOOK

According to the U.S. Department of Labor, employment of market and survey research workers is expected to grow faster than the average for all occupations through 2014. Job opportunities should be ample for those trained in public opinion research, particularly those with graduate degrees. Those who specialize in marketing, mathematics, and statistics will have the best opportunities. Marketing research firms, financial services organizations, health care institutions, advertising firms, and insurance firms are potential employers.

FOR MORE INFORMATION

For more information on market research, contact
Advertising Research Foundation
432 Park Avenue South
New York, NY 10016-8013
Tel: 212-751-5656
Email: info@thearf.org
http://www.thearf.org

For information on graduate programs, contact
American Association for Public Opinion Research
PO Box 14263
Lenexa, KS 66285-4263
Tel: 913-310-0118
Email: AAPOR-info@goAMP.com
http://www.aapor.org

For career development information, contact
American Marketing Association
311 South Wacker Drive, Suite 5800
Chicago, IL 60606-6629
Tel: 800-262-1150
Email: info@ama.org
http://www.marketingpower.com

For comprehensive information on market and opinion research, contact
Council for Marketing and Opinion Research
110 National Drive, 2nd Floor
Glastonbury, CT 06033-1212
Tel: 860-657-1881
Email: information@cmor.org
http://www.cmor.org

For information on survey research and graduate programs, contact
Council of American Survey Research Organizations
170 North Country Road, Suite 4
Port Jefferson, NY 11777-2606
Tel: 631-928-6954
Email: casro@casro.org
http://www.casro.org

For career information, contact
Marketing Research Association
110 National Drive, 2nd Floor
Glastonbury, CT 06033-1212
Tel: 860-682-1000
Email: email@mra-net.org
http://www.mra-net.org

The following companies are leaders in survey and marketing research.
The Gallup Organization
http://www.gallup.com

Harris Interactive
http://www.harrisinteractive.com

Reporters

OVERVIEW

Reporters are the foot soldiers for newspapers, magazines, and television and radio broadcast companies. They gather and analyze information about current events and write stories for publication or for broadcasting. News analysts, reporters, and correspondents hold approximately 64,000 jobs in the United States.

HISTORY

Newspapers are the primary disseminators of news in the United States. People read newspapers to learn about the current events that are shaping their society and societies around the world. Newspapers give public expression to opinion and criticism of government and societal issues, and, of course, provide the public with entertaining, informative reading.

Newspapers are able to fulfill these functions because of the freedom given to the press. However, this was not always the case. The first American newspaper, published in 1690, was suppressed four days after it was published. And it was not until 1704 that the first continuous newspaper appeared.

One early newspaperman who later became a famous writer was Benjamin Franklin. Franklin worked for his brother at a Boston newspaper before publishing his own paper two years later in 1723 in Philadelphia.

A number of developments in the printing industry made it possible for newspapers to be printed more cheaply. In the late 19th century, new types of presses were developed to increase production, and more importantly, the Linotype machine was invented. The Linotype mechanically set letters so that handset type was no longer necessary.

A high school journalism student interviews her principal for a story in the school newspaper. *(The Image Works)*

This dramatically decreased the amount of prepress time needed to get a page into print. Newspapers could respond to breaking stories more quickly, and late editions with breaking stories became part of the news world.

These technological advances, along with an increasing population, factored into the rapid growth of the newspaper industry in the United States. In 1776, there were only 37 newspapers in the United States. Today there are more than 1,450 daily and more than 6,700 weekly newspapers in the country.

As newspapers grew in size and widened the scope of their coverage, it became necessary to increase the number of employees and to assign them specialized jobs. Reporters have always been the heart of newspaper staffs. However, in today's complex world, with the public hungry for news as it occurs, reporters and correspondents are involved in all media—not only newspapers, but magazines, radio, and television as well. Today, with the advent of the Internet, many newspapers have gone online, causing many reporters to become active participants on the Information Superhighway.

THE JOB

Reporters collect information on newsworthy events and prepare stories for newspaper or magazine publication or for radio or television broadcast. The stories may simply provide information about local, state, or national events, or they may present opposing points of view on issues of current interest. In this latter capacity, the press plays an important role in monitoring the actions of public officials and others in positions of power.

Stories may originate as an assignment from an editor or as the result of a lead, or news tip. Good reporters are always on the lookout for good story ideas. To cover a story, they gather and verify facts by interviewing people involved in or related to the event, examining documents and public records, observing events as they happen, and researching relevant background information. Reporters generally take notes or use a tape recorder as they collect information and write their stories once they return to their offices. In order to meet a deadline, they may have to telephone the stories to *rewriters,* who write or transcribe the stories for them. After the facts have been gathered and verified, the reporters transcribe their notes, organize their material, and determine what emphasis, or angle, to give the news. The story is then written to meet prescribed standards of editorial style and format.

The basic functions of reporters are to observe events objectively and impartially, record them accurately, and explain what the news means in a larger, societal context. Within this framework, there are several types of reporters.

The most basic is the *news reporter.* This job sometimes involves covering a beat, which means that the reporter may be assigned to consistently cover news from an area such as the local courthouse, police station, or school system. It may involve receiving general assignments, such as a story about an unusual occurrence or an obituary of a community leader. Large daily papers may assign teams of reporters to investigate social, economic, or political events and conditions.

Many newspaper, wire service, and magazine reporters specialize in one type of story, either because they have a particular interest in the subject or because they have acquired the expertise to analyze and interpret news in that particular area. *Topical reporters* cover stories for a specific department, such as medicine, politics, foreign affairs, sports, consumer affairs, finance, science, business, education, labor, or religion. They sometimes write features explaining the history that has led up to certain events in the field they cover. *Feature writers* generally write longer, broader stories than news reporters, usually on more upbeat subjects, such as fashion, art, theater, travel, and social events. They may write about trends, for example, or profile local celebrities. *Editorial writers* and *syndicated news columnists* present viewpoints that, although based on a thorough knowledge, are opinions on topics of popular interest. *Columnists* write under a byline and usually specialize in a particular subject, such as politics or government activities. (For more information on this career, see the article "Columnists.") *Critics* review restaurants, books, works of art, movies, plays, musical performances, and other cultural events.

Specializing allows reporters to focus their efforts, talent, and knowledge on one area of expertise. It also gives them more opportunities to develop deeper relationships with contacts and sources, which is necessary to gain access to the news.

Correspondents report events in locations distant from their home offices. They may report news by mail, telephone, fax, or computer from rural areas, large cities throughout the United States, or countries. Many large newspapers, magazines, and broadcast companies have one correspondent who is responsible for covering all the news for the foreign city or country where they are based. These reporters are known as *foreign correspondents*. (For more information on this career, see the article "Foreign Correspondents.")

Reporters on small or weekly newspapers not only cover all aspects of the news in their communities, but also may take photographs, write editorials and headlines, layout pages, edit wire-service copy, and help with general office work.

REQUIREMENTS

High School

High school courses that will provide you with a firm foundation for a reporting career include English, journalism, history, social studies, communications, typing, and computer science. Speech courses will help you hone your interviewing skills, which are necessary for success as a reporter. In addition, it will be helpful to take college prep courses, such as foreign language, math, and science.

Postsecondary Training

You will need at least a bachelor's degree to become a reporter, and a graduate degree will give you a great advantage over those entering the field with lesser degrees. Most editors prefer applicants with degrees in journalism because their studies include liberal arts courses as well as professional training in journalism. Some editors consider it sufficient for a reporter to have a good general education from a liberal arts college. Others prefer applicants with an undergraduate degree in liberal arts and a master's degree in journalism. The great majority of journalism graduates hired today by newspapers, wire services, and magazines have majored specifically in news-editorial journalism.

More than 400 colleges offer programs in journalism leading to a bachelor's degree. In these schools, around three-fourths of a student's time is devoted to a liberal arts education and one-fourth to the professional study of journalism, with required courses such as introductory mass media, basic reporting and copy editing, history of journalism, and press law and ethics. Students are encouraged to select other journalism courses according to their specific interests.

Journalism courses and programs are also offered by many community and junior colleges. Graduates of these programs are prepared to go to work directly as general assignment reporters, but they may encounter difficulty when competing with graduates of four-year programs. Credit earned in community and junior colleges may be transferable to four-year programs in journalism at other colleges and universities. Journalism training may also be obtained in the armed forces. Names and addresses of newspapers and a list of journalism schools and departments are published in the annual *Editor & Publisher International Year Book: The Encyclopedia of the Newspaper Industry* (New York: Editor & Publisher) which is available for reference in most public libraries and newspaper offices.

A master's degree in journalism may be earned at approximately 120 schools, and a doctorate at about 35 schools. Graduate degrees may prepare students specifically for careers in news or as journalism teachers, researchers, and theorists, or for jobs in advertising or public relations.

A reporter's liberal arts training should include courses in English (with an emphasis on writing), sociology, political science, economics, history, psychology, business, speech, and computer science. Knowledge of foreign languages is also useful. To be a reporter in a specialized field, such as science or finance, requires concentrated course work in that area.

Other Requirements

In order to succeed as a reporter, it is crucial that you have typing skill, as you will type your stories using word processing programs. Although not essential, a knowledge of shorthand or speedwriting makes note taking easier, and an acquaintance with news photography is an asset.

You must also be inquisitive, aggressive, persistent, and detail-oriented. You should enjoy interacting with people of various races, cultures, religions, economic levels, and social statuses.

EXPLORING

You can explore a career as a reporter in a number of ways. You can talk to reporters and editors at local newspapers. You can interview the admissions counselor at the school of journalism closest to your home.

In addition to taking courses in English, journalism, social studies, speech, computer science, and typing, high school students can acquire practical experience by working on school newspapers or on a church, synagogue, or mosque newsletter. Part-time and summer jobs on newspapers provide invaluable experience to the aspiring reporter.

College students can develop their reporting skills in the laboratory courses or workshops that are part of the journalism curriculum. College students might also accept jobs as campus correspondents for selected newspapers. People who work as part-time reporters covering news in a particular area of a community are known as *stringers* and are paid only for those stories that are printed.

More than 3,000 journalism scholarships, fellowships, and assistantships are offered by universities, newspapers, foundations, and professional organizations to college students. Many newspapers and magazines offer summer internships to journalism students to provide them with practical experience in a variety of basic reporting and editing duties. Students who successfully complete internships are usually placed in jobs more quickly upon graduation than those without such experience.

EMPLOYERS

Of the approximately 64,000 reporters and correspondents employed in the United States, approximately 61 percent work for newspaper, periodical, book, and directory publishers. About 25 percent work in radio and television broadcasting. The rest are employed by wire services.

STARTING OUT

Jobs in this field may be obtained through college career services offices or by applying directly to the personnel departments of individual employers. If you have some practical experience, you will have an advantage; you should be prepared to present a portfolio of material you wrote as a volunteer or part-time reporter, or other writing samples.

Most journalism school graduates start out as general assignment reporters or copy editors for small publications. A few outstanding journalism graduates may be hired by large city newspapers or national magazines. They are trained on the job. But they are the exception, as large employers usually require several years' experience. As a rule, novice reporters cover routine assignments, such as reporting on civic and club meetings, writing obituaries, or summarizing speeches. As you become more skilled in reporting, you will be assigned to more important events or to a regular beat, or you may specialize in a particular field.

ADVANCEMENT

Reporters may advance by moving to larger newspapers or press services, but competition for such positions is unusually keen. Many highly qualified reporters apply for these jobs every year.

A select number of reporters eventually become columnists, correspondents, editorial writers, editors, or top executives. These important and influential positions represent the top of the field, and competition is strong for them.

Many reporters transfer the contacts and knowledge developed in newspaper reporting to related fields, such as public relations, advertising, or preparing copy for radio and television news programs.

EARNINGS

There are great variations in the earnings of reporters. Salaries are related to experience, the type of employer for which the reporter works, geographic location, and whether the reporter is covered by a contract negotiated by the Newspaper Guild.

According to the U.S. Department of Labor, the median salary for reporters and correspondents was $32,270 in 2005. The lowest paid 10 percent of these workers earned $18,300 or less per year, while the highest paid 10 percent made $71,220 or more annually. Mean annual earnings for reporters employed in newspaper, book, and directory publishing were $36,770 in 2005; reporters employed in Internet publishing had mean annual earnings of $41,940.

According to the Newspaper Guild, the top minimum salary for reporters with about five years' experience under guild contracts ranged from $27,130 to $72,130 or more.

WORK ENVIRONMENT

Reporters work under a great deal of pressure in settings that differ from the typical business office. Their jobs generally require a five-day, 35- to 40-hour week, but overtime and irregular schedules are very common. Reporters employed by morning papers start work in the late afternoon and finish around midnight, while those on afternoon or evening papers start early in the morning and work until early or mid-afternoon. Foreign correspondents often work late at night to send the news to their papers in time to meet printing deadlines.

The day of the smoky, ink-stained newsroom has passed, but newspaper offices are still hectic places. Reporters have to work amid the clatter of computer keyboards and other machines, loud voices engaged in telephone conversations, and the bustle created by people hurrying about. An atmosphere of excitement prevails, especially as press deadlines approach.

Travel is often required in this occupation, and some assignments may be dangerous, such as covering wars, political uprisings, fires, floods, and other events of a volatile nature.

OUTLOOK

Employment for reporters and correspondents is expected to grow more slowly than the average for all occupations through 2014, according to the *Occupational Outlook Handbook*. While the number of self-employed reporters and correspondents is expected to grow, newspaper jobs are expected to decrease because of mergers, consolidations, and closures in the newspaper industry.

Because of an increase in the number of small community and suburban daily and weekly newspapers, opportunities will be best for journalism graduates who are willing to relocate and accept relatively low starting salaries. With experience, reporters on these small papers can move up to editing positions or may choose to transfer to reporting jobs on larger newspapers or magazines.

Openings will be limited on big city dailies. While individual papers may enlarge their reporting staffs, little or no change is expected in the total number of these newspapers. Applicants will face strong competition for jobs on large metropolitan newspapers. Experience is a definite requirement, which rules out most new graduates unless they possess credentials in an area for which the publication has a pressing need. Occasionally, a beginner can use contacts and experience gained through internship programs and summer jobs to obtain a reporting job immediately after graduation.

A significant number of jobs will be provided by magazines, but the major news magazines generally prefer experienced reporters. Stronger employment growth is expected for reporters in online newspapers and magazines.

Overall, the prospects are best for graduates who have majored in news-editorial journalism and completed an internship while in school. The top graduates in an accredited program will have a great advantage, as will talented technical and scientific writers. Small newspapers prefer to hire beginning reporters who are acquainted with the community and are willing to help with photography and other aspects of production. Without at least a bachelor's degree in journalism, applicants will find it increasingly difficult to obtain even an entry-level position.

Those with doctorates and practical reporting experience may find teaching positions at four-year colleges and universities, while highly qualified reporters with master's degrees may obtain employment in journalism departments of community and junior colleges.

Poor economic conditions do not drastically affect the employment of reporters and correspondents. Their numbers are not severely cut back even during a downturn; instead, employers forced to reduce expenditures will suspend new hiring.

FOR MORE INFORMATION

For a list of accredited programs in journalism and mass communications, visit the ACEJMC's Web site
Accrediting Council on Education in Journalism and Mass
Communications (ACEJMC)
University of Kansas School of Journalism and Mass
Communications
Stauffer-Flint Hall, 1435 Jayhawk Boulevard
Lawrence, KS 66045-7575
Tel: 785-864-3973
http://www.ku.edu/~acejmc/STUDENT/PROGLIST.shtml

This organization provides general educational information on all areas of journalism.
Association for Education in Journalism and Mass Communication
234 Outlet Pointe Boulevard
Columbia, SC 29210-5667
Tel: 803-798-0271
http://www.aejmc.org

To read The Journalist's Road to Success: A Career Guide, *which lists schools offering degrees in news-editing, and financial aid to those interested in print journalism, visit the DJNF's Web site*
Dow Jones Newspaper Fund (DJNF)
PO Box 300
Princeton, NJ 08543-0300
Tel: 609-452-2820
Email: newsfund@wsj.dowjones.com
http://djnewspaperfund.dowjones.com

For information on investigative journalism, contact
Investigative Reporters and Editors
Missouri School of Journalism
138 Neff Annex
Columbia, MO 65211-0001
Tel: 573-882-2042
Email: info@ire.org
http://www.ire.org

For information on careers in newspapers and industry facts and figures, contact
Newspaper Association of America
4401 Wilson Boulevard, Suite 900
Arlington, VA 22203-1867
Tel: 571-366-1000
Email: IRC@naa.org
http://www.naa.org

For information on union membership, contact
Newspaper Guild-Communication Workers of America
501 Third Street, NW
Washington, DC 20001-2797
Tel: 202-434-7177
http://www.newsguild.org

Contact the society for information on student chapters, scholarships, educational information, discussion groups, and much more.
Society of Professional Journalists
Eugene S. Pulliam National Journalism Center
3909 North Meridian Street
Indianapolis, IN 46208-4011
Tel: 317-927-8000
http://www.spj.org

Visit the following Web site for comprehensive information on journalism careers, summer programs, and college journalism programs.
High School Journalism
http://www.highschooljournalism.org

For comprehensive information for citizens, students, and news people about the field of journalism, visit
Project for Excellence in Journalism
http://www.journalism.org

INTERVIEW

Julie Deardorff is a health and fitness reporter for the Chicago Tribune. *(To read her work, visit http://www.chicagotribune.com.) She discussed her career with the editors of* Careers in Focus: Newspapers.

Q. Why did you decide to become a reporter?

A. In fourth grade I started journaling after reading *The Diary of Anne Frank* and *Harriet the Spy*, and I still journal to this day. That's when I decided I was going to be a writer. In seventh grade, when we had to do a report on careers, I looked up "writer" and the profession listed was "reporter." That was all it took (I guess I was fairly impressionable), and after I learned about the profession, I never thought I would do anything else.

Q. Take us through a day in your life as a health/fitness reporter. What are your typical tasks/responsibilities?

A. I read several daily health news digests that select stories from across the world, read the wires, comb through endless e-mail pitches from public relations sources, and check into all the major journals to see what new studies are coming out and what studies are embargoed for later in the week. I get out when I can, but generally do most of my interviewing by phone or e-mail. I'm responsible for a weekly column, a (usually) daily health-related blog entry (though my Internet work is considered separate from print), stories for the Tuesday health section of Tempo [a section of the *Tribune*], and cover stories for a Sunday feature section called "Q."

Q. What do you like most and least about your job?

A. Health and fitness is a personal interest so it makes it much easier to get excited about the topics I'm writing about. I love that I often talk to the most knowledgeable people in the field about a subject. I also love when I write something that has a positive impact on someone's life.

My least favorite part is dealing with those who believe their view is the only correct one and who object to presenting alternative ideas about health. Pharmaceutical drugs and surgery are not the only solutions to health problems.

Q. What advice would you give to high school students? who are interested in becoming reporters?

A. The same advice people gave me. Keep a journal. Read as much as possible. And write like crazy. It's also critical to get experience. I started as a sportswriter for our local paper when I was in high school. If I were in school now, I wouldn't pursue print journalism—I would focus on Internet-based reporting.

Science and Medical Writers

OVERVIEW

Science and medical writers translate technical medical and scientific information so it can be disseminated to the general public and professionals in the field. Science and medical writers research, interpret, write, and edit scientific and medical information. Their work often appears in books, technical studies and reports, magazine and trade journal articles, newspapers, company newsletters, and on Web sites and may be used for radio and television broadcasts.

HISTORY

The skill of writing has existed for thousands of years. Papyrus fragments with writing by ancient Egyptians date from about 3000 B.C., and archaeological findings show that the Chinese had developed books by about 1300 B.C. A number of technical obstacles had to be overcome before printing and the writing profession progressed.

The modern publishing age began in the 18th century. Printing became mechanized, and the novel, magazine, and newspaper developed. Developments in the printing trades, photoengraving, retailing, and the availability of capital produced a boom in newspapers and magazines in the 19th century. Further mechanization in the printing field, such as the use of the Linotype machine, high-speed rotary presses, and special color-reproduction processes, set the stage for still further growth in the book, newspaper, and magazine industry.

QUICK FACTS

School Subjects
Biology
English
Journalism

Personal Skills
Communication/ideas
Technical/scientific

Work Environment
Primarily indoors
Primarily multiple locations

Minimum Education Level
Bachelor's degree

Salary Range
$24,320 to $46,000 to $89,940+

Certification or Licensing
Voluntary

Outlook
About as fast as the average

DOT
131

GOE
01.02.01

NOC
5121

O*NET-SOC
27-3042.00, 27-3043.00

The broadcasting industry has also contributed to the development of the professional writer. Film, radio, and television are sources of entertainment, information, and education that provide employment for thousands of writers. Today, the computer industry and Internet Web sites have also created the need for more writers.

As our world becomes more complex and people seek even more information, professional writers have become increasingly important. And, as medicine and science take giant steps forward and discoveries are being made every day that impact our lives, skilled science and medical writers are needed to document these changes and disseminate the information to the general public and more specialized audiences.

THE JOB

Science and medical writers usually write about subjects related to these fields. Because the medical and scientific subject areas may sometimes overlap, writers often find that they do science writing as well as medical writing. For instance, a medical writer might write about a scientific study that has an impact on the medical field.

Science and medical writers usually write for the general public. They translate high-tech information into articles and reports that the general public and the media can understand. Good writers who cover the subjects thoroughly have inquisitive minds and enjoy looking for additional information that might add to their articles. They research the topic to gain a thorough understanding of the subject matter. This may require hours of research on the Internet, or in corporate, university, or public libraries. Writers always need good background information regarding a subject before they can write about it.

In order to get the information required, writers may interview professionals such as doctors, pharmacists, scientists, engineers, managers, and others who are familiar with the subject. Writers must know how to present the information so it can be understood. This requires knowing the audience and how to reach them. For example, an article may need graphs, photos, or historical facts. Writers sometimes enlist the help of technical or medical illustrators or engineers in order to add a visual dimension to their work.

For example, if reporting on a new heart surgery procedure that will soon be available to the public, writers may need to illustrate how that surgery is performed and what areas of the heart are affected. They may give a basic overview of how the healthy heart works, show a diseased heart in comparison, and report on how this surgery can help the patient. The public will also want to know how many people are affected by this disease, what the symptoms are, how many procedures have been done successfully, where they were performed, what the recovery time is, and if there are any complications. In addition, interviews with doctors and patients add a personal touch to the story.

Writers usually need to work quickly because news-related stories are often deadline-oriented. Because science and medicine can be so complex, science and medical writers also need to help the audience understand and evaluate the information. Writing for the Web encompasses most journalistic guidelines including time constraints and sometimes space constraints.

Some science and medical writers specialize in their subject matter. For instance, a medical writer may write only about heart disease and earn a reputation as the best writer in that subject area. Science writers may limit their writing or research to environmental science subjects, or may be even more specific and focus only on air pollution issues.

According to Jeanie Davis, president of the Southeast Chapter of the American Medical Writers Association, "Medical writing can take several different avenues. You may be a consumer medical writer, write technical medical research, or write about health care issues. Some choose to be medical editors and edit reports written by researchers. Sometimes this medical research must be translated into reports and news releases that the public can understand. Today many writers write for the Web." Davis adds, "It is a very dynamic profession, always changing."

"This career can have various appeals," says Barbara Gastel, M.D., coordinator of the master of science program in science and technology journalism at Texas A&M University. "People can combine their interest in science or medicine with their love of writing. It is a good field for a generalist who likes science and doesn't want to be tied to research in one area. Plus," she adds, "it is always fun to get things published."

Some writers may choose to be freelance writers either on a full- or part-time basis, or to supplement other jobs. Freelance science and medical writers are self-employed writers who work with small and large companies, health care organizations, research institutions, or publishing firms on a contract or hourly basis. They may specialize in writing about a specific scientific or medical subject for one or two clients, or they may write about a broad range of subjects for a number of different clients. Many freelance writers write articles, papers, or reports and then attempt to get them published in newspapers, trade, or consumer publications.

REQUIREMENTS

High School

If you are considering a career as a writer, you should take English, journalism, and communication courses in high school. Computer classes will also be helpful. If you know in high school that you want to do scientific or medical writing, it would be to your advantage to take biology, physiology, chemistry, physics, math, health, psychology, and other science-related courses. If your school offers journalism courses and you have the chance to work on the school newspaper or yearbook, you should take advantage of these opportunities. Part-time employment at health care facilities, newspapers, publishing companies, or scientific research facilities can also provide experience and insight regarding this career. Volunteer opportunities are also available in hospitals and nursing homes.

Postsecondary Training

Although not all writers are college-educated, today's jobs almost always require a bachelor's degree. Many writers earn an undergraduate degree in English, journalism, or liberal arts and then obtain a master's degree in a communications field such as medical or science writing. A good liberal arts education is important since you are often required to write about many subject areas. Science and medical-related courses are highly recommended. You should investigate internship programs that give you experience in the communications department of a corporation, medical institution, or research facility. Some newspapers, magazines, or public relations firms also have internships that give you the opportunity to write.

Some people find that after working as a writer, their interests are strong in the medical or science fields and they evolve into that writing specialty. They may return to school and enter a master's degree program or take some additional courses related specifically to science and medical writing. Similarly, science majors or people in the medical fields may find that they like the writing aspect of their jobs and return to school to pursue a career as a medical or science writer.

Certification or Licensing

Certification is not mandatory; however, certification programs are available from various organizations and institutions. The American Medical Writers Association offers educational workshops leading to core or advanced curriculum certificates.

Other Requirements

If you are considering a career as a medical or science writer, you should enjoy writing, be able to write well, and be able to express your ideas and those of others clearly. You should have an excellent knowledge of the English language and have superb grammar and spelling skills. You should be skilled in research techniques and be computer literate and familiar with software programs related to writing and publishing. You should be curious, enjoy learning about new things, and have an interest in science or medicine. You need to be detail-oriented since many of your writing assignments will require that you obtain and relay accurate and detailed information. Interpersonal skills are also important because many jobs require that you interact with and interview professional people such as scientists, engineers, researchers, and medical personnel. You must be able to meet deadlines and work under pressure.

EXPLORING

As a high school or college student, you can test your interest and aptitude in the field of writing by serving as a reporter or writer on school newspapers, yearbooks, and literary magazines. Attending writing workshops and taking writing classes will give you the opportunity to practice and sharpen your skills.

Community newspapers often welcome contributions from outside sources, although they may not have the resources to pay for them. Jobs in bookstores, magazine shops, libraries, and even newsstands offer a chance to become familiar with various publications. If you are interested in science writing, try to get a part-time job in a research laboratory, interview science writers, and read good science writing in major newspapers such as the *New York Times* or the *Wall Street Journal*. Similarly, if your interest is medical writing, work or volunteer in a health care facility, visit with people who do medical writing, and read medical articles in those newspapers previously listed. You may also find it helpful to read publications such as the *American Medical Writers Association Journal*. For more information visit http://www.amwa.org.

Information on writing as a career may also be obtained by visiting local newspapers and publishing houses and interviewing some of the writers who work there. Career conferences and other guidance programs frequently include speakers from local or national organizations who can provide information on communication careers.

Some professional organizations such as the Society for Technical Communication welcome students as members and have special student membership rates and career information. In addition, participation in professional organizations gives you the opportunity to meet and visit with people in this career field.

EMPLOYERS

Many science and medical writers are employed, often on a freelance basis, by newspaper, magazine, and book publishers and the broadcast industries as well. Internet publishing is a growing field that hires science and medical writers.

Other employers of medical writers include pharmaceutical and drug companies, medical research institutions, government organizations, insurance companies, health care facilities, nonprofit organizations, medical publishers, medical associations, and other medical-related industries.

Science writers may also be employed by medical-related industries. In addition, they are employed by scientific research companies, government research facilities, federal, state, and local agencies, manufacturing companies, research and development departments of corporations, and the chemical industries. Large universities and hospitals often employ science writers. Large technology-based corporations and industrial research groups also hire science writers.

STARTING OUT

A fair amount of experience is required to gain a high-level position in this field. Most writers start out in entry-level positions. These jobs may be listed with college career services offices, or you may apply directly to the employment departments of publishing companies, corporations, institutions, universities, research facilities, nonprofit organizations, and government facilities that hire science and medical writers. Many firms now hire writers directly upon application or recommendation of college professors and career services offices. Want ads in newspapers and trade journals are another source for jobs. Serving an internship in college can give you the advantage of knowing people who can give you personal recommendations.

Internships are also excellent ways to build your portfolio. Employers in the communications field are usually interested in seeing samples of your published writing assembled in an organized portfolio or scrapbook. Working on your college's magazine or newspaper staff can help you build a portfolio. Sometimes small, regional or local magazines and newspapers will also buy articles or assign short pieces for you to write. You should attempt to build your portfolio with good writing samples. Be sure to include the type of writing you are interested in doing, if possible.

You may need to begin your career as a junior writer or editor and work your way up. This usually involves library research, preparation of rough drafts for part or all of a report, cataloging, and other related writing tasks. These are generally carried on under the supervision of a senior writer.

Many science and medical writers enter the field after working in public relations departments, the medical profession, or science-related industries. They may use their skills to transfer to specialized writing positions or they may take additional courses or graduate work that focuses on writing or documentation skills.

ADVANCEMENT

Writers with only an undergraduate degree may choose to earn a graduate degree in science or medical writing, corporate communications, document design, or a related program. An advanced degree may open doors to more progressive career options.

Many experienced science and medical writers are often promoted to head writing, documentation, or public relations departments within corporations or institutions. Some may become recognized experts in their field and their writings may be in demand by trade journals, newspapers, magazines, and the broadcast industry. Writers employed by newspapers and magazines may advance by working for larger, more prestigious publications.

As freelance writers prove themselves and work successfully with clients, they may be able to demand increased contract fees or hourly rates.

EARNINGS

Although there are no specific salary studies for science and medical writers, salary information for all writers is available. The U.S. Department of Labor reports that the mean annual salary for writers employed by newspaper, book, and directory publishers in 2005 was $47,590. Salaries for all writers ranged from less than $24,320 to more than $89,940. Mean annual earnings for technical writers employed by newspaper, book, and directory publishers were $45,270 in 2005. The lowest 10 percent of all technical writers earned less than $33,250, while the highest 10 percent earned more than $87,550.

According to the Society for Technical Communication, the median salary for technical writers and editors in the United States was $60,240 in 2006.

Freelance writers' earnings can vary depending on their expertise, reputation, and the articles they are contracted to write.

Most full-time writing positions offer the usual benefits such as insurance, sick leave, and paid vacation. Some jobs also provide tuition reimbursement and retirement benefits. Freelance writers must pay for their own insurance. However, there are professional associations that may offer group insurance rates for its members.

WORK ENVIRONMENT

Work environment depends on the type of science or medical writing and the employer. Generally, writers work in an office or research environment. Writers for the news media sometimes work in noisy surroundings. Some writers travel to research information and conduct interviews while other employers may confine research to local libraries or the Internet. In addition, some employers require writers to conduct research interviews over the phone, rather than in person.

Although the workweek usually runs 35 to 40 hours in a normal office setting, many writers may have to work overtime to cover a story, interview people, meet deadlines, or to disseminate information in a timely manner. The newspaper industry delivers the news 24 hours a day, seven days a week. Writers often work nights and weekends to meet press deadlines or to cover a late-developing story.

Each day may bring new and interesting situations. Some stories may even take writers to exotic locations with a chance to interview

Learn More About It

Friedlander, Edward Jay, and John Lee. *Feature Writing for Newspapers and Magazines: The Pursuit of Excellence.* 5th ed. Boston: Allyn & Bacon, 2003.
Goldberg, Jan. *Careers in Journalism.* 3d ed. New York: McGraw-Hill, 2005.
McKinney, Anne. *Real-Resumes for Media, Newspaper, Broadcasting and Public Affairs Jobs: Including Real Resumes Used to Change Careers and Transfer Skills to Other Industries.* Fayetteville, N.C.: Prep Publishing, 2002.
Meyer, Philip. *The Vanishing Newspaper: Saving Journalism In The Information Age.* Columbia: University of Missouri Press, 2004.
Peter, Roy and Christopher Scanlan. (eds.) *America's Best Newspaper Writing: A Collection of ASNE Prizewinners.* 2d ed. Boston: Bedford/St. Martin's, 2005.
Sova, Dawn B. *How to Write Articles for Newspapers and Magazines.* 2d ed. Lawrenceville, N.J.: ARCO, 2002.

famous people and write about timely topics. Other assignments may be boring or they may take place in less than desirable settings, where interview subjects may be rude and unwilling to talk. One of the most difficult elements for writers may be meeting deadlines or gathering information. People who are the most content as writers work well with deadline pressure.

OUTLOOK

According to the U.S. Department of Labor, there is strong competition for writing and editing jobs, and growth in writing careers should occur at an average rate through 2014. Opportunities will be very good for science and medical writers, as continued developments in these fields will drive the need for skilled writers to put complex information in terms that a wide and varied audience can understand.

FOR MORE INFORMATION

For information on a career as a medical writer, contact
American Medical Writers Association
40 West Gude Drive, Suite 101
Rockville, MD 20850-1192
Tel: 301-294-5303
Email: amwa@amwa.org
http://www.amwa.org

To read advice for beginning science writers, visit the NASW's Web site
National Association of Science Writers (NASW)
PO Box 890
Hedgesville, WV 25427-0890
Tel: 304-754-5077
http://www.nasw.org

For information on scholarships and student memberships aimed at those preparing for a career in technical communication, contact
Society for Technical Communication
901 North Stuart Street, Suite 904
Arlington, VA 22203-1822
Tel: 703-522-4114
Email: stc@stc.org
http://www.stc.org

Sportswriters

OVERVIEW

Sportswriters cover the news in sports for newspapers and magazines. They research original ideas or follow up on breaking stories, contacting coaches, athletes, and team owners and managers for comments or more information. Sometimes a sportswriter is fortunate enough to get his or her own column, in which the sportswriter editorializes on current news or developments in sports.

HISTORY

For as long as sports have been played and newspapers and magazines have been published, there has been a demand for sportswriters to report the scores, detail the game winning plays of the day, and otherwise provide coverage of athletes, teams, and sports competitions. Sportswriters are employed by both newspapers and magazines throughout the United States and the world.

THE JOB

The sportswriter's primary job is to report the outcomes of the sports events that occurred that day. Since one newspaper can't employ enough reporters to cover, in person, every single high school, college, and professional sports event that happens on any given day, let alone sports events happening in other cities and countries, sportswriters use the wire news services to get the details. Major national and international wire services include Reuters, Associated Press, United Press International, Agence France-Presse, and ITAR-Tass. The entire body of statistics for tennis matches, hockey games, and track-and-field events, for example, can be sent over the wire

QUICK FACTS

School Subjects
English
Journalism
Physical education

Personal Skills
Communication/ideas

Work Environment
Indoors and outdoors
Primarily multiple locations

Minimum Education Level
Bachelor's degree

Salary Range
$24,320 to $47,950 to $89,940+

Certification or Licensing
None available

Outlook
About as fast as the average

DOT
131

GOE
11.08.03

NOC
5231

O*NET-SOC
27-3043.02

service so that sportswriters can include the general story and the vital statistics in as condensed or lengthy a form as space allows.

A sportswriter begins work each day by reviewing the local, national, and international news that comes in over the wire news services. He or she then begins researching the top or lead stories to try to flesh out the story, perhaps with a local perspective on it, or to come up with a new angle or spin, altogether. An example of a lead story might be the comeback of a professional tennis star; the underdog victory of a third-rate, much-maligned football team; the incredible pitching record of a high school athlete; or the details of a football running back who blew out his knee in a crucial last-minute play. The sportswriter then calls or interviews in person coaches, athletes, scouts, agents, promoters, and sometimes, in the case of an athletic injury, a physician or team of physicians.

The next step for the sportswriter is to write the story. Most sportswriters for newspapers are subject to the constraints of space, and these limits can change in a matter of minutes. On a dull day, up until the hour before the paper is published, the sportswriter might have a quarter of a page to fill with local sports news. At the last minute, however, an entire Super Bowl team could come down with food poisoning, in which case the sports editor would probably want to cover this larger, breaking story. To accommodate the new articles about the poisoning, the effect on team morale, whether or not the Super Bowl might be postponed for the first time in history, the local sports coverage would either have to shrink considerably or be completely cut. To manage this, sportswriters, like other reporters who write for daily newspapers, compose their stories with the most crucial facts contained within the first one or two paragraphs of the story. They may write a 10-paragraph story, but if it had to be shortened, the pertinent information would be easily retained.

Even with the help of news services, sportswriters still couldn't have all the sports news at their fingertips without the help of other reporters and writers, known in the world of reporting as *stringers*. A stringer covers an event that, most likely, would not be covered by the wire services, events such as high school sports events, as well as games in professional sports that are occurring simultaneously with other major sports events. The stringer attends the sports event and phones in scores, or e-mails or faxes in a complete report.

Sportswriters for newspapers typically only cover a particular sport, such as baseball. Others are assigned a beat, or specific area, and like other reporters must cover all the events that fall into that beat. For example, a sportswriter assigned to the high school football beat for a newspaper in Los Angeles, California, would be expected to cover all the area high school football games. Since football is seasonal, he or she might be assigned to the high school basketball beat during the winter season. On the other hand, the sportswriter working in Lexington, Kentucky, might be assigned coverage of all the high school sports in the area, not simply one sport. Much of the way in which assignments are given depends on experience as well as budget and staffing constraints.

REQUIREMENTS

High School

English, journalism, and speech are the most important classes for you to take in high school. You will need to master the art of writing in order to convey your ideas concisely, yet creatively, to your readers. Speech classes will help you become comfortable interacting with others. Be sure to take physical education classes and participate in organized sports, be it as a competitor, a team manager, or an assistant. You also should join the staff of your school paper or yearbook. This will give you a chance to cover and write about your school's sports teams or other school activities.

Postsecondary Training

You will need at least a bachelor's degree to become a sportswriter, although many sportswriters go on to study journalism at the graduate level. Most sportswriters concentrate on journalism while in college, either by attending a program in journalism or by taking whatever courses are available outside of a specialized program. This isn't to say that you can't become a sportswriter without a degree in journalism, but competition for sportswriting jobs is incredibly fierce. After all, sportswriters get great seats at sports events, and they have the credentials to get them into interviews with sports celebrities. Increasingly, a specialized education is becoming the means by which sports editors and managers sift through the stacks of resumes from prospective sportswriters. Sportswriters may have degrees in communications or English, among other majors.

Other Requirements

Clearly, the ability to write well and concisely is another requirement for the job of the sportswriter. In addition, you must have a solid understanding of the rules and play of many different sports. If you hope to specialize in the coverage of one particular sport, your knowledge of that sport has to be equal to that of anyone coaching or playing it at the professional level.

Finally, you must be able to elicit information from a variety of sources, as well as to determine when information being leaked is closer to promotional spin than to fact. There will be more times when a coach or agent will not want to comment on a story than the times when they will want to make an on-the-record comment, so the sportswriter must be assertive in pressing the source for more information.

EXPLORING

You can learn on-the-job skills by working for your high school and college papers. The experience can be related to sports, of course, but any journalistic experience will help you develop the basic skills useful to any reporter, regardless of the area about which you are writing.

You can increase your chances and success in the field by applying to colleges or universities with renowned academic programs in journalism. Most accredited programs have a required period of training in which you will intern with a major newspaper somewhere in the United States; student interns are responsible for covering a beat.

You may also find it helpful to read the sports section of your local newspaper or other publications that are related to this field, such as *Sports Illustrated* (http://sportsillustrated.cnn.com) and *Sports Business Journal* (http://www.sportsbusinessjournal.com), and visit Web sites such as the Associated Press Sports Editors (http://apse. dallasnews.com).

EMPLOYERS

Sportswriters are employed by newspapers, magazines, and Web sites throughout the world. They may cover professional teams based in large cities or high school teams located in tiny towns. Sportswriters also work as freelance writers.

STARTING OUT

You may have to begin your career as a sportswriter by covering the games or matches that no else wants to or can cover. As a stringer, you won't earn much money, you'll probably have a second or even third job, but eventually it may lead to covering bigger and better games and teams. Some sportswriters make a living out of covering sports for very small towns, others only work at those jobs until they have gained the experience to move on.

Most journalists start their careers by working in small markets—little towns and cities with local papers. You may work for a newspaper for a year or two and then apply for positions with larger

papers in bigger towns and cities. Sportswriters for newspapers follow the same routine, and more than a few end up pursuing areas
other than sports because the job openings in sports simply weren't
there. The lucky few who hang on to a small sports beat can often
parlay that beat into a better position by sticking with the job and
demonstrating a devotion to the sport, even cultivating a following
of loyal fans. This could lead to a full-time column.

Most likely, as a sportswriter, you will take advantage of opportunities to learn more about athletes and sports in general. Becoming
an expert on a little-known but rapidly growing sport may be one
way for you to do this. For example, if you were to learn all that you
can about mountain biking, you might be able to land a job with one
of the publications specializing in the sport of mountain biking.

The career services offices of colleges or universities with accredited undergraduate and graduate programs in journalism can be
extremely helpful in beginning your job search. In fact, many graduates of these programs are not only highly sought after by newspapers and magazines, but these graduates are often offered jobs by
the newspapers and magazines with which they had an internship
during school.

ADVANCEMENT

The constraints of budget, staffing, and time—which make a sportswriters' job difficult—are also often what can help a sportswriter
rise through the ranks. For example, the writer asked to cover all
the sports in a small area may have to hustle to cover the beat alone,
but that writer also won't have any competition when covering the
big events. Thus, he or she can gain valuable experience and bylines
writing for a small paper, whereas in a larger market, the same
sportswriter would have to wait much longer to be assigned an event
that might result in a coveted byline.

Sportswriters advance by gaining the top assignments, covering
the major sports in feature articles, as opposed to the bare bones
summaries of events. They also advance by moving to larger and
larger papers, by getting columns, and finally, by getting a syndicated column—that is, a column carried by many papers around the
country or even around the world.

In the publishing worlds of both newspapers and magazines,
sportswriters can advance by becoming editors of a newspaper's
sports page or of a sports magazine. There are also *sports publicists*
and *sports information directors* who work for the publicity and
promotions arms of colleges, universities, and professional sports
teams. These individuals release statements, write and disseminate

Learn More About It

---------------. *All American Sports IQ Test: Ultimate Playbook of Trivia, Teasers and Puzzles*. New York: Sporting News Books, 2004.

Aamidor, Abraham. *Real Sports Reporting*. Bloomington, Ind.: Indiana University Press, 2003.

Andrews, Phil. *Sports Journalism: A Practical Introduction*. Thousand Oaks, Calif.: Sage Publications Ltd., 2005.

Eskenazi, Gerald. *A Sportswriter's Life: From the Desk of a New York Times Reporter*. Columbia: University of Missouri Press, 2004.

Lewis, Michael. (ed.) *The Best American Sports Writing 2006*. Boston: Houghton Mifflin, 2006.

Staten, Vince. *Why Is The Foul Pole Fair?: Answers to 101 of the Most Perplexing Baseball Questions*. New York: Simon & Schuster, 2004.

Tibballs, Geoff. *The Olympics' Strangest Moments: Extraordinary But True Tales From The History Of The Olympic Games*. London, U.K.: Robson Books, 2005.

Walsh, Christopher J. *No Time Outs: What It's Really Like to Be a Sportswriter Today*. Lanham, Md.: Taylor Trade Publishing, 2006.

Wilstein, Steve. *Associated Press Sports Writing Handbook*. New York: McGraw-Hill, 2001.

to the press articles on the organizations' teams and athletes, and arrange press opportunities for coaches and athletes.

EARNINGS

According the U.S. Department of Labor, writers had median annual earnings of $46,420 in 2005. The lowest 10 percent earned less than $24,320, while the highest 10 percent earned more than $89,940. The mean annual salary (for all writers) in the newspaper industry was $47,950.

Sportswriters who cover the major sports events, who have their own column, or who have a syndicated column can expect to earn more than the salaries above.

WORK ENVIRONMENT

Like other journalists, sportswriters work in a variety of conditions, from the air-conditioned offices of a newsroom or magazine publisher to the sweaty, humid locker room of a professional basketball team, to the arid and dusty field where a baseball team's spring training is held. Sportswriters work irregular hours, putting in as much or as little time as the story requires, often traveling to small towns and out-of-the-way locales to cover a team's away games.

The benefits are obvious: For the individuals who love sports, the job offers the chance to cover sports events every day, to immerse themselves in the statistics and injury lists and bidding wars of professional and amateur sports, and to speak, sometimes one-on-one, with talented athletes.

OUTLOOK

The turnover rate for top sportswriters with major newspapers isn't very high, which means that job openings occur as sportswriters retire, die, are fired, or move into other markets. While the publishing industry may have room in it for yet another magazine devoted to a particular sports specialty, competition for sportswriting jobs will continue to be strong into 2014 and beyond.

FOR MORE INFORMATION

The AWSM is a membership organization of women and men employed in sports writing, editing, broadcast and production, public relations, and sports information. Visit its Web site for information on internships and scholarships.

Association for Women in Sports Media (AWSM)
PO Box F
Bayville, NJ 08721-0317
http://www.awsmonline.org

Associated Press Sports Editors is a membership organization that strives to improve print journalistic standards in sports newsrooms. Web site visitors will find up-to-date news articles regarding industry happenings, a job board, and a downloadable monthly newsletter, as well as links to Web sites for all of the major professional sports organizations and leagues. Membership information, including an in-depth profile of the organization, is also included.

Associated Press Sports Editors
c/o The Dallas Morning News: Sports Day
508 Young Street
Dallas, TX 75202-4808
Tel: 214-977-8222
http://apse.dallasnews.com

Founded in 1958 by The Wall Street Journal *to improve the quality of journalism education, this organization offers internships, scholarships, and literature for college students.* To read The Journalist's Road to Success: A Career Guide, *which lists schools offering degrees in news-editing, and financial aid to those interested in print journalism, visit the DJNF's Web site.*

Dow Jones Newspaper Fund (DJNF)
PO Box 300
Princeton, NJ 08543-0300
Tel: 609-452-2820
Email: newsfund@wsj.dowjones.com
http://djnewspaperfund.dowjones.com

Career information, including a pamphlet called Facts about Newspapers, *is available from*
Newspaper Association of America
4401 Wilson Boulevard, Suite 900
Arlington, VA 22203-1867
Tel: 571-366-1000
http://www.naa.org

For information on careers and salaries in the newspaper industry, contact
The Newspaper Guild-CWA (Communications Workers of America)
501 Third Street, NW, Suite 250
Washington, DC 20001-2797
Tel: 202-434-7177
http://www.newsguild.org

Writers

OVERVIEW

Writers express, edit, promote, and interpret ideas and facts in written form for newspapers, books, magazines, trade journals, technical studies and reports, company newsletters, radio and television broadcasts, and advertisements.

Writers develop fiction and nonfiction ideas for plays, novels, poems, and other related works; report, analyze, and interpret facts, events, and personalities; review art, music, film, drama, and other artistic presentations; and persuade the general public to choose or favor certain goods, services, and personalities. There are approximately 192,000 salaried writers, authors, and technical writers employed in the United States.

HISTORY

The skill of writing has existed for thousands of years. Papyrus fragments with writing by ancient Egyptians date from about 3000 B.C., and archaeological findings show that the Chinese had developed books by about 1300 B.C. A number of technical obstacles had to be overcome before printing and the profession of writing evolved. Books of the Middle Ages were copied by hand on parchment. The ornate style that marked these books helped ensure their rarity. Also, few people were able to read. Religious fervor prohibited the reproduction of secular literature.

The development of the printing press by Johannes Gutenberg in the middle of the 15th century and the liberalism of the Protestant Reformation, which encouraged a wide range of publications, greater literacy, and the creation of a number of works of literary

QUICK FACTS

School Subjects
English
Journalism

Personal Skills
Communication/ideas
Helping/teaching

Work Environment
Primarily indoors
Primarily one location

Minimum Education Level
Bachelor's degree

Salary Range
$24,320 to $47,950 to $89,940+

Certification or Licensing
None available

Outlook
About as fast as the average

DOT
131

GOE
01.01.02

NOC
5121

O*NET-SOC
27-3043.00

New York Times reporter and writer Alex Kuczynski speaks to a fan at the Texas Book Festival in Austin. *(The Image Works)*

merit, prompted the development of the publishing industry. The first authors worked directly with printers.

The modern publishing age began in the 18th century. Printing became mechanized, and the novel, magazine, and newspaper developed. The first newspaper in the American colonies appeared in the early 18th century, but it was Benjamin Franklin who, as editor and writer, made the *Pennsylvania Gazette* one of the most influential in setting a high standard for his fellow American journalists. Franklin also published the first magazine in the colonies, *The American Magazine,* in 1741.

Advances in the printing trades, photoengraving, retailing, and the availability of capital produced a boom in newspapers and magazines in the 19th century. Further mechanization in the printing field, such as the use of the Linotype machine, high-speed rotary presses, and special color reproduction processes, set the stage for still further growth in the book, newspaper, and magazine industry.

In addition to the print media, the broadcasting industry has contributed to the development of the professional writer. Film, radio, and television are sources of entertainment, information, and education that provide employment for thousands of writers.

THE JOB

Writers work in the field of communications. Specifically, they deal with the written word, whether it is destined for the printed page, broadcast, computer screen, or live theater. The nature of their work is as varied as the materials they produce: newspapers, books, magazines, trade journals, technical reports, company newsletters and other publications, advertisements, speeches, scripts for motion picture and stage productions, and scripts for radio and television broadcast. Writers develop ideas and write for all media.

Prose writers for newspapers, magazines, and books share many of the same duties. First they come up with an idea for an article or book from their own interests or are assigned a topic by an editor. The topic is of relevance to the particular publication. (For example, a writer for a newspaper with a regular section on parenting may be assigned an article on car seat safety.) Then writers begin gathering as much information as possible about the subject through library research, interviews, the Internet, observation, and other methods. They keep extensive notes from which they draw material for their project. Once the material has been organized and arranged in logical sequence, writers prepare a written outline. The process of developing a piece of writing is exciting, although it can also involve detailed and solitary work. After researching an idea, a writer might discover that a different perspective or related topic would be more effective, entertaining, or marketable.

When working on assignment, writers submit their outlines to an editor or other company representative for approval. Then they write a first draft of the manuscript, trying to put the material into words that will have the desired effect on their audience. They often rewrite or polish sections of the material as they proceed, always searching for just the right way of imparting information or expressing an idea or opinion. A manuscript may be reviewed, corrected, and revised numerous times before a final copy is submitted. Even after that, an editor may request additional changes.

Writers for newspapers, magazines, or books often specialize in their subject matter. Some writers might have an educational background that allows them to give critical interpretations or analyses.

For example, a health or science writer for a newspaper typically has a degree in biology and can interpret new ideas in the field for the average reader.

Columnists or *commentators* analyze news and social issues. (For more information on this career, see the article "Columnists.") They write about events from the standpoint of their own experience or opinion. *Critics* review literary, musical, or artistic works and performances. *Editorial writers* write on topics of public interest, and their comments, consistent with the viewpoints and policies of their employers, are intended to stimulate or mold public opinion. *Newswriters* work for newspapers, radio, or TV news departments, writing news stories from notes supplied by reporters or wire services.

Corporate writers and writers for nonprofit organizations have a wide variety of responsibilities. These writers may work in such places as a large media company or for a small nonprofit religious group, where they may be required to write news releases, annual reports, speeches for the company president, or public relations materials. Typically they are assigned a topic with length requirements for a given project. They may receive raw research materials, such as statistics, and they are expected to conduct additional research, including personal interviews. These writers must be able to write quickly and accurately on short deadlines, while also working with people whose primary job is not in the communications field. The written work is submitted to a supervisor and often a legal department for approval; rewrites are a normal part of this job.

Copywriters write copy that is primarily designed to sell goods and services. Their work appears as advertisements in newspapers, magazines, and other publications or as commercials on radio and television broadcasts. Sales and marketing representatives first provide information on the product and help determine the style and length of the copy. The copywriters conduct additional research and interviews; to formulate an effective approach, they study advertising trends and review surveys of consumer preferences. Armed with this information, copywriters write a draft that is submitted to the account executive and the client for approval. The copy is often returned for correction and revision until everyone involved is satisfied. Copywriters, like corporate writers, may also write articles, bulletins, news releases, sales letters, speeches, and other related informative and promotional material. Many copywriters are employed in advertising agencies. They also may work for public relations firms or in communications departments of large companies.

Writers can be employed either as in-house staff or as freelancers. Pay varies according to experience and the position, but freelancers must provide their own office space and equipment such as computers and fax machines. Freelancers also are responsible for keeping tax records, sending out invoices, negotiating contracts, and providing their own health insurance.

REQUIREMENTS
High School
While in high school, build a broad educational foundation by taking courses in English, literature, foreign languages, history, general science, social studies, computer science, and typing. The ability to type is almost a requisite for all positions in the communications field, as is familiarity with computers.

Postsecondary Training
Competition for writing jobs almost always demands the background of a college education. Many employers prefer you have a broad liberal arts background or majors in English, literature, history, philosophy, or one of the social sciences. Other employers—especially newspaper and book publishers—desire communications or journalism training in college. Occasionally a master's degree in a specialized writing field may be required. A number of schools offer courses in journalism, and some of them offer courses or majors in book publishing, publication management, and newspaper and magazine writing.

In addition to formal course work, most employers look for practical writing experience. If you have served on high school or college newspapers, yearbooks, or literary magazines, or if you have worked for small community newspapers or radio stations, even in an unpaid position, you will be an attractive candidate. Many newspapers, book publishers, magazines, and radio and television stations have summer internship programs that provide valuable training if you want to learn about the publishing and broadcasting businesses. Interns do many simple tasks, such as running errands and answering phones, but some may be asked to perform research, conduct interviews, or even write some minor pieces.

Writers who specialize in technical fields may need degrees, concentrated course work, or experience in specific subject areas. This applies frequently to engineering, business, or one of the sciences. Also, technical communications is a degree now offered at many universities and colleges.

If you wish to enter positions with the federal government, you will have to take a civil service examination and meet certain specified requirements, according to the type and level of position.

Other Requirements

To be a writer, you should be creative and able to express ideas clearly, have a broad general knowledge, be skilled in research techniques, and be computer literate. Other assets include curiosity, persistence, initiative, resourcefulness, and an accurate memory. For some jobs—on a newspaper, for example, where the activity is hectic and deadlines are short—the ability to concentrate and produce under pressure is essential.

EXPLORING

As a high school or college student, you can test your interest and aptitude in the field of writing by serving as a reporter or writer on school newspapers, yearbooks, and literary magazines. Various writing courses and workshops will provide the opportunity to sharpen your writing skills.

Small community newspapers and local radio stations often welcome contributions from outside sources, although they may not have the resources to pay for them. Jobs in bookstores, magazine shops, and even newsstands will offer you a chance to become familiar with various publications.

You can also obtain information on writing as a career by visiting local newspapers and publishers and interviewing some of the writers who work there. Career conferences and other guidance programs frequently include speakers on the entire field of communications from local or national organizations.

EMPLOYERS

There are approximately 142,000 writers and authors and 50,000 technical writers currently employed in the United States. Approximately half of salaried writers and editors work in the information sector, which includes newspapers, magazines, book publishers, radio and television broadcasting, software publishers, and Internet businesses. Writers also work for advertising agencies and public relations firms and work on journals and newsletters published by business and nonprofit organizations, such as professional associations, labor unions, and religious organizations. Other employers are government agencies and film production companies.

STARTING OUT

A fair amount of experience is required to gain a high-level position in the field. Most writers start out in entry-level positions. These jobs may be listed with college career services offices, or they may be obtained by applying directly to the employment departments of the individual publishers or broadcasting companies. Graduates who previously served internships with these companies often have the advantage of knowing someone who can give them a personal recommendation. Want ads in newspapers and trade journals are another source for jobs. Because of the competition for positions, however, few vacancies are listed with public or private employment agencies.

Employers in the communications field usually are interested in samples of published writing. These are often assembled in an organized portfolio or scrapbook. Bylined or signed articles are more credible (and, as a result, more useful) than stories whose source is not identified.

Entry-level positions as a junior writer usually involve library research, preparation of rough drafts for part or all of a report, cataloging, and other related writing tasks. These are generally carried on under the supervision of a senior writer.

ADVANCEMENT

Most writers find their first jobs as editorial or production assistants. Advancement may be more rapid in small companies, where beginners learn by doing a little bit of everything and may be given writing tasks immediately. In large firms, duties are usually more compartmentalized. Assistants in entry-level positions are assigned such tasks as research, fact checking, and copyrighting, but it generally takes much longer to advance to full-scale writing duties.

Promotion into more responsible positions may come with the assignment of more important articles and stories to write, or it may be the result of moving to another company. Mobility among employees in this field is common. An assistant in one publishing house may switch to an executive position in another. Or a writer may switch to a related field as a type of advancement.

Freelance or self-employed writers earn advancement in the form of larger fees as they gain exposure and establish their reputations.

EARNINGS

In 2005, median annual earnings for salaried writers and authors were $46,420 a year, according to the U.S. Department of Labor. The lowest 10 percent earned less than $24,320, while the highest 10 percent earned $89,940 or more.

In addition to their salaries, many writers earn some income from freelance work. Part-time freelancers may earn from $5,000 to

$15,000 a year. Freelance earnings vary widely. Full-time established freelance writers may earn more than $75,000 a year.

WORK ENVIRONMENT

Working conditions vary for writers. Although their workweek usually runs 35 to 40 hours, many writers work overtime. A publication that is issued frequently has more deadlines closer together, creating greater pressures to meet them. The work is especially hectic on newspapers, which operate seven days a week. Writers often work nights and weekends to meet deadlines or to cover a late-developing story.

Most writers work independently, but they often must cooperate with artists, photographers, rewriters, and advertising people who may have widely differing ideas of how the materials should be prepared and presented.

Physical surroundings range from comfortable private offices to noisy, crowded newsrooms filled with other workers typing and talking on the telephone. Some writers must confine their research to the library or telephone interviews, but others may travel to other cities or countries or to local sites, such as theaters, ballparks, airports, factories, or other offices.

The work is arduous, but most writers are seldom bored. Some jobs, such as that of the foreign correspondent, require travel. The most difficult element is the continual pressure of deadlines. People who are the most content as writers enjoy and work well with deadline pressure.

OUTLOOK

The employment of writers is expected to increase at an average rate through 2014, according to the U.S. Department of Labor. Competition for writing jobs has been and will continue to be competitive. The demand for writers by newspapers, periodicals, book publishers, and nonprofit organizations is expected to increase. The growth of online publishing on company Web sites and other online services will also create a demand for many talented writers; those with computer skills will be at an advantage as a result. Advertising and public relations will also provide job opportunities.

The major book and magazine publishers, broadcasting companies, advertising agencies, public relations firms, and the federal government account for the concentration of writers in large cities such as New York, Chicago, Los Angeles, Boston, Philadelphia,

San Francisco, and Washington, D.C. Opportunities with small newspapers, corporations, and professional, religious, business, technical, and trade publications can be found throughout the country.

People entering this field should realize that the competition for jobs is extremely keen. Beginners may have difficulty finding employment. Of the thousands who graduate each year with degrees in English, journalism, communications, and the liberal arts, intending to establish a career as a writer, many turn to other occupations when they find that applicants far outnumber the job openings available. College students would do well to keep this in mind and prepare for an unrelated alternate career in the event they are unable to obtain a position as writer; another benefit of this approach is that, at the same time, they will become qualified as writers in a specialized field. The practicality of preparing for alternate careers is borne out by the fact that opportunities are best in firms that prepare business and trade publications and in technical writing. Job candidates with good writing skills and knowledge of a specialized area such as economics, finance, computer programming, or science will have the best chances of finding jobs.

Potential writers who end up working in a different field may be able to earn some income as freelancers, selling articles, stories, books, and possibly TV and movie scripts, but it is usually difficult for writers to support themselves entirely on independent writing.

FOR MORE INFORMATION

For information on careers in newspaper reporting, education, and financial aid opportunities, contact

American Society of Journalists and Authors
1501 Broadway, Suite 302
New York, NY 10036-5505
Tel: 212-997-0947
http://www.asja.org

This organization provides general educational information on all areas of journalism, including newspapers, magazines, television, and radio.

Association for Education in Journalism and Mass Communication
234 Outlet Pointe Boulevard
Columbia, SC 29210-5667
Tel: 803-798-0271
http://www.aejmc.org

For information on science writing and editing, contact
National Association of Science Writers
PO Box 890
Hedgesville, WV 25427-0890
Tel: 304-754-5077
http://www.nasw.org

This organization offers student memberships for those interested in opinion writing.
National Conference of Editorial Writers
3899 North Front Street
Harrisburg, PA 17110-1583
Tel: 717-703-3015
Email: ncew@pa-news.org
http://www.ncew.org

For comprehensive information on the newspaper industry, contact
Newspaper Association of America
4401 Wilson Boulevard, Suite 900
Arlington, VA 22203-1867
Tel: 571-366-1000
Email: IRC@naa.org
http://www.naa.org

Index